Make Money & Have Fun

"When Fred and I jumped on our second call I was shocked to see how far he'd progressed in such a short time. Beyond just a writer, Fred's entrepreneurial endeavors will lead him to much prosperity!"

~**David Hancock**, Founder of Morgan James Publishing

"Fred Posimo is ahead of his time and full of wisdom, not to mention a great and very funny guy!"

~**Brian Meara**, Founder of Investor Entourage

"Fred Posimo is a prodigy. Whatever he puts his mind to he excels at and he has the mindset to get you on the path to success. Grab this book now!"

~**Ken McArthur**, Best-Selling Author and Producer

"Fred is one of the few people who have come into the industry and taken as much action in bettering himself and his business along the way. There are many who preach what they want and their vision, but Fred is someone who does what it takes to become the best at his craft. I'm honored to know someone who will become a great leader in this industry for others to follow."

~**Dan Zitofsky**, Founder of Passive Wealth Academy

"Fred Posimo is one of the few people I've seen who instantly applies what he learns. His ability to take action is one of his greatest qualities. Success is definitely in his future!"

~**Nick Tang**, Real Estate Investor/ Meetup Mogul

"Fred has the mindset of a champion. He has a ton of wisdom to share about what it takes to succeed at a high level. Fred's tips, tactics, & techniques to making money and having fun will help entrepreneurs take their business & life to the next level."

~**Tim Bratz**, CEO, Legacy Wealth Holdings

"If you are trying to rebuild your life… or start your business… *Make Money and Have Fun!* by Fred Posimo is a MUST READ!!!"

~**Les Brown**

"Fred is a great human being! He is always looking for ways to further his education and his sphere of influence. Fred practices what he preaches."

~**Ramsey Coulter**, Credit Expert

"Make Money & Have Fun is a Must Read! Fred Posimo is a budding superstar with a winning mindset! His philosophies and principles he shares in this book will grow your business and your life!"

~**Sir John Shin**, Executive Producer, Think & Grow Rich The Legacy

"When I invited Fred Posimo to my private estate I instantly recognized his potential! This young and hungry entrepreneur has truly separated himself from the 95% who only dream of success to the 5% who actually achieve it! Grab a copy of Make Money & Have Fun now it might just change your life!"

~**Dr. Greg S. Reid**, Award Winning Author & Filmmaker

MAKE MONEY

**Bridge the Gap Between
Your Passion and Prosperity**

FRED POSIMO

NEW YORK

LONDON • NASHVILLE • MELBOURNE • VANCOUVER

Make Money & Have Fun

Bridge the Gap Between Your Passion and Prosperity

Published in New York, New York, by Morgan James Publishing. Morgan James is a trademark of Morgan James, LLC. www.MorganJamesPublishing.com

Proudly distributed by Ingram Publisher Services

A **FREE** ebook edition is available for you
or a friend with the purchase of this print book.

CLEARLY SIGN YOUR NAME ABOVE

Instructions to claim your free ebook edition:
1. Visit MorganJamesBOGO.com
2. Sign your name CLEARLY in the space above
3. Complete the form and submit a photo
   of this entire page
4. You or your friend can download the ebook
   to your preferred device

ISBN 9781631955129 paperback
ISBN 9781631955136 ebook
Library of Congress Control Number:
2021931078

Cover & Interior Design by:
Christopher Kirk
www.GFSstudio.com

Morgan James is a proud partner of Habitat for Humanity Peninsula
and Greater Williamsburg. Partners in building since 2006.

Get involved today! Visit MorganJamesPublishing.com/giving-back

DEDICATION

To my Soulmate and Partner in Crime Hannah Spolidoro,
you are my source of everything
and my inspiration to continue on each day!

TABLE OF CONTENTS

ACKNOWLEDGMENTS

So many people deserve to be mentioned here, too many to count, many who directly impacted the publication and success of this book, others less directly. Words are a poor medium through which to express my full gratitude for these individuals. However, I shall try my best.

To David Hancock and the entire Morgan James Publishing team, you are each amazing individuals, and I am thankful to be publishing with you. Equally, Ken McArthur deserves recognition here for introducing me to David, and thus the spiral unraveled. Larry Steinhouse and Phil Falcone at Investor Schooling, thank you for being there at the most opportune time and for opening the doors to so many more connections.

Many thanks to Manny Lopez, a loyal and worthy coach. To Les Brown, for being a hero in the hearts of many including mine. To Greg Reid, for opening up your home and your network. To every guest on my syndicated show, including: Ely Delaney, Dan Zitofsky, Brian Meara, Ramsey Coulter, Alec

Stern, Gene McNaughton, Sir John Shin, John Lee Dumas and all the others. To Lana McAra and everyone else I met at that first mastermind. To all of my past karate instructors for paving the way of my future.

But of all these people I need to acknowledge one individual who stands out in my mind among the rest, Patrick Shanahan, my Junior year entrepreneurship teacher. You opened my mind in ways I never imagined possible. From 17 years old, I developed an insatiable desire to learn and grow in business, and I thank you for igniting this spark in me.

In closing, I need to acknowledge my family, Mom, Dad, Jess, Mike, Scarlett and Shadow. You have been there through it all (or at least most of it), and it has made all the difference. To my beautiful girlfriend and soulmate Hannah Spolidoro, I look forward to living a life with you, and I am thankful you've stuck by me this long. Thank you all. You are all incredible human beings, and you each deserve more than I can put into words. Just know that you have impacted my life along with many others.

FOREWORD

Hi. My name is Les Brown, international motivational speaker and trainer. I have been blessed to travel the globe sharing my story of overcoming the odds to encourage others to live their dreams despite their circumstances.

I have lived. I have earned. Now it is time to pass it on. I believe that success leaves clues. Certain rules have allowed me to achieve success. That is why it is important to study the habits of successful people. If you are looking to tap into your own inner potential… If you are trying to rebuild your life… or start your business… *Make Money & Have Fun!* by Fred Posimo is a MUST READ!!!

Make Money & Have Fun! is a blueprint for building a life that is both fulfilling and lucrative. Fred takes you step by step to creating the life you seek. He starts with the most essential element to changing your life, which is your mindset. Mr. Posimo speaks in very simple and concise terms. He teaches concepts such as, "No one rises to low expectations. You have to break out of mediocre belief systems and embrace your unique gifts and talents." He teaches about the importance of celebrating being you and mastering your skills and talents. This book provides thought-provoking questions to help you find out what your passion is. Fred helps you discover what you love to do, then how to monetize what you love to do.

Sustained success is achieved when you do an inventory of all aspects of your life Physical, Mental, Emotional, Spiritual and Financial. *Make Money & Have Fun!* gives you action steps to transforming your life.

One the most important things about having success in life is enjoying yourself. Life is not about the destination but the growth and development you gain on your journey. The best part of my work is: It's not work. It's my passion. I am not working. I am having fun! This book reinforces the importance of having fun, without fun it won't be worth the hard work and effort. Ultimately, this book is a guide on how to get rich and have fun while doing it for dummies from A-Z. If you are looking to go from living a life of mediocrity to manifesting massive success! *Make Money & Have Fun!* is the book for you. You have greatness within you! That is my story and I am sticking to it.

~Les Brown

INTRODUCTION

The wealthy 1% think differently than the rest of the world, and early-on, I had a burning desire to learn those differences. In my own journey to financial success, I eventually discovered the answer, and it is incredibly simple... but not easy.

The thought processes of the wealthy involve multiple facets including understanding the difference between "High Financial Literacy" and "Low Financial Literacy," recognizing, and utilizing "The 4 Currencies," establishing an idea that this planet is supported, not by gravity but instead by 5 very distinct Pillars and, of course, learning the Number One key to all success.

See, financial problems are often not caused by a lack of money. They're caused by an abundance of money with most people not having a clue about what to do with it! In that regard, "High Financial Literacy" is not connected to how much net worth or income someone has.

Many sports superstars and movie celebrities earn millions of dollars, but most have Low Financial Literacy and squander their income on liabilities. A bankrupt truck driver might have zero dollars at that moment, but after some training, he can soon learn how to create cashflow and keep more of his money. His financial potential is lightyears ahead of those with Low Financial Literacy, regardless of his cash on hand.

Another key discovery I made is that there are more currencies on this earth beyond money used all around the globe. In fact, there are 4 currencies, or mediums of exchange. This new knowledge creates a leverageable scenario where you can flip, skip and arbitrage your way to achieving your financial results in ways you likely never knew were possible. For instance, you can use these currencies to create strong partnerships where each person leverages their contributions creating a synergy of real value that can be measured.

As I uncovered these financial truths, I realized this journey involved more than just how to make money. Countless stories arise of "miserable millionaires," individuals who have achieved unfathomable financial heights, yet wake up every day feeling unfulfilled, plague our world.

I didn't want to end up that way. So, I asked myself the question: how can I make money and have fun at the same time? The answer lies in asking the right questions in the right way and paying attention to how you feel throughout your day. When you feel anxious, stressed, or overwhelmed, that is often a sign to make a change. Using the EAD Filter along with many of the additional exercises in this book, I will show you how to overcome minor setbacks and transform your trials into triumphs!

Can you imagine living a life of financial fulfillment where time flies by and you feel a rush when you think about the next day? Can you imagine watching your bank account grow while simultaneously having the time of your life? If something inside you is giving a nod, then this book is for you.

Turn the page, and you'll catch a vision of a world where you can play in your sweet spot, watch your income rise and live fully aligned. It's time to Make Money and Have Fun!

~ Fred Posimo

SECTION 1

Mindset Makeover

Chapter 1

ROUND PEGS, SQUARE PEGS

A re you a Round Peg or a Square Peg? Not sure? Your answer could hold the key to your success. An easy way to discover which type you are is by looking at your track record in school.

My dad and I often enjoy lively discussions about the modern school system. Somehow, we started using round pegs and square pegs to describe two types of students:

1. **Round Pegs: Are** Students who excel in school and often show proficiency in their classwork, homework, tests and assignments. In the classroom, they are well behaved, have high GPAs and generally seem right at home. Round Pegs never seem overwhelmed nor stressed and they don't tend to struggle, whether their task is big or small. They fit perfectly into a round hole (a.k.a. the school system).

2. **Square Pegs: Are** students who struggle in school and perform poorly on classwork, homework, tests and assignments. School often feels tedious and/or frustrating to them and, they're distracted, bored, disruptive and talkative. In short, these students generally either shut down or misbehave all day long and they often appear withdrawn or overwhelmed, frustrated and out of place. They don't fit into the round hole (the school system) at all.

"They don't fit into the round hole (the school system) at all."

The reality is the structured rigidity of the classic American school system sets up many students for failure, and it has left far too many believing they are failures. The problem is not whether a student is a "Round Peg" or a "Square Peg"; the problem is the school's response to them. Most schools only teach to one type of students: the Round pegs . They seem to assume that anyone who doesn't fit perfectly into their Round Hole system must be "broken" or have something wrong with them. Before a Square Peg student leaves their institution, the system will work relentlessly to force them into conforming with the Round Holes, to chip off the corners and "fix them" so they will fit like everybody else.

Me, I'm a Square Peg. I remember in grade school feeling like an outcast and an oddball. On nearly a daily basis I was ostracized and bullied by fellow classmates. As the grades progressed these feelings never dissipated. At first I thought "What's wrong with me? Why can't this just come naturally to me, why can't I "fit in" like everybody else?" Around the start of high school, I began to look at my "shortcomings" as superpowers! The question changed to: "What if this obstacle is my greatest opportunity, what if I am the way I am for a reason?" It was also around this time I began noticing parallels outside of the classroom as well. For instance, I was never a sports person, but I love martial arts, instead of going out on the weekends I stayed in and studied personal development and money. Generally, as a human I often made uncommon, unique, and "off the beaten path" choices throughout my life. When I finally embraced being a square peg my life began to change. My obstacles transformed into opportunities, the moments that made me feel like a misfit or out of place seemed to disappear. I fully stepped into my power and realized who I was as a human being and most importantly what I had to give, that is one of the reasons why you hold this book in your hands right now.

When young children struggle to fit in at school, this often leads to a progressively negative domino effect throughout their life. Their personal perception of self-worth diminishes and can even disappear entirely. This likely could have been my reality had I not stepped into my full potential as a young teenager.

This "Round Peg, Square Peg" Philosophy carries over into other areas of life beyond just school. There are round pegs and Square pegs everywhere on this planet. The round pegs typically follow the beaten path, they do as they're told, follow the rules, and generally live a predictable routine. Square pegs will typically be more adventurous, spontaneous, and mavericks who chart their own course and make their own way. In short, their life is more spontaneous and less predictable. When these square pegs step into their superpower and accept who they are, like I did in high school, they'll find their place in this world. Unfortunately, school performance often remains the defining factor of how most people see themselves, and it can influence all of their other experiences throughout life. Poor grades can deter future business owners, derail aspiring artists, and unravel a soon-to-be investors potential. These individuals often begin doubting whether they are capable or worthy in this world, because they aren't excelling in what has been told is the most critical thing for them: the school system.

As the host of my weekly mastermind I discovered that most of my successful entrepreneur members are Square Pegs who have been shamed, blamed and disrespected at the most vulnerable time in their lives—when they were growing up. To become successful, they had to overcome their setbacks, change their mindset and understand their value to the world, separate from traditional measures like grades and test scores.

"Most successful entrepreneurs I know are Square Pegs."

Wrestling vs. Jiu-Jitsu

The world subscribes to one of two principles found in a philosophy which I call wrestling vs. jiu-jitsu. As a practitioner of both (wrestling in high school and about 5 years of jiu-jitsu) I found very subtle yet distinct similarities and differences between them relating to mindset.

The wrestling philosophy says, "Pick a move, and if that move doesn't work, keep doing it harder until it does." Jiu-jitsu says, "Pick a move, and if that move doesn't work, keep trying others until you find the best approach." From the standpoint of watching a match, the two approaches look the same, yet this subtle difference causes a massive change in your results.

Applying this to the school system, one could say the school system's philosophy is, "If you are a Square Peg, we'll chisel you down until you conform and become a Round Peg. We'll keep hitting you harder until we force you to become round by the time you leave." They build a wall around your life and punish you for trying to climb it. School systems subscribe to a wrestling philosophy. In everyday life we might often subscribe to a similar "grin and bear it" mentality where we are a poor fit but we work hard and relentlessly to force ourselves to succeed. I'm not saying that hard work isn't crucial to success, but there is a better approach than pushing yourself into it. The jiu-jitsu approach will deliver far better outcomes for far more students.

"They build a wall around your life and punish you for trying to climb it."

I find it interesting that colleges sort through their applicants looking for Round Pegs. They aren't interested in Square Pegs. If a Square Peg does slip through their sorting office—known as admissions—the institution immediately goes into the chipping process. Once again, the Square Peg is presented with the message that they aren't good enough as they are, so they will either conform, fail or leave. This goes beyond college with beliefs like: "work harder," "fake it til you make it," and "push yourself!" I'm here to challenge these beliefs. *Make Money and Have Fun* is about creating alignment between your prosperity and your passion so you can live financially fulfilled and truly bridge that gap without needing to force yourself to do so!

> *"We cannot solve our problems with the same thinking we*
> *used when we created them."*
> ~Albert Einstein

We've all heard of Bill Gates and Steve Jobs leaving college to pursue their dreams. They slipped through the sorting machine and got accepted, but Steven Spielberg didn't get that far. He was turned down twice for a film course at the University of Southern California and instead attended community college. He got his start by landing an unpaid position in the editing department at Universal Studios. While there, he wrote and directed a short film that won several awards. At that point, an executive noticed Spielberg's talent and signed him to a seven-year directing contract making him the youngest director to land a long-term contract with a major studio.

Forbes' Most Influential Celebrities in 2014 listed Spielberg as the most influential celebrity in America. His net worth is about 3.7 Billion.

Some might say, "What a shame that Spielberg wasn't admitted to film school," but I would reply, "What a close call."

Joan Crawford starred in *The Twilight Zone* episode that marked Spielberg's debut as a studio director when he was twenty-one years old. In her biography, *Not the Girl Next Door*, Crawford said,

> *It was immediately obvious to me, and probably everyone else,*
> *that here was a young genius. I thought maybe more experience*
> *was important, but then I thought of all of those experienced*
> *directors who didn't have Steven's intuitive inspiration and who*

just kept repeating the same old routine performances. That was called "experience.[1]

Is it possible that film-school training might have chipped off Spielberg's square edges, and he would have ended up in mediocrity? Who can say for sure?

Soichiro Honda grew up in a village in Japan. He hated school and eventually dropped out. As a result, he had no formal education. He left home at age fifteen and went to Tokyo where he worked as an apprentice in an auto repair garage. Six years later, he returned to his village and started his own garage. He was twenty-two years old.

Then, he began tinkering with motorized bicycles. He designed and mass-produced an engine and then his own motorized bicycle. In 1949 he produced his first motorcycle and opened his first U.S. dealership in 1959. Honda Motorcycles became a billion-dollar global company that also developed the cars we recognize today. In 1989, he was inducted into the Automotive Hall of Fame.

Malcolm Gladwell talks of "outliers," who are basically the Square Pegs described in this chapter. Gladwell agrees that the Square Pegs are the change-makers who forge a path to a new and better future!

> "Square Pegs are the change-makers
> who forge a path to a new and better future!"

---

1   Chandler, Charlotte. *Not the Girl Next Door: Joan Crawford, a Personal Biography*, Hal Leonard Corp. (2008) p. 261

School isn't the only institution that tries to force people to fit in. The military, some religions, certain athletic or sports programs—and even individuals such as overbearing parents, mentors, employers or coaches—can prescribe to the forcing route, demanding conformity, which usually creates limiting beliefs and negative mindsets in a young person. Without help to break free from these negative mindsets, they can last a lifetime. My philosophy: "If you're a Square Peg, here's a garden of square holes. Let's figure out where you fit best and train you to succeed there." Think of this book as your roadmap to alignment. Put into practice the methods and techniques in this book and you'll find yourself financially fulfilled in no time! My journey started this way. At 18 years old I went on a reading escapade and read over a dozen books on personal development and self-improvement. Because of that, today I own and run multiple businesses, I've become friends with multi-millionaires and wake up everyday making money and having fun, now it's your turn!

"If you're a Square Peg, here's a garden of square holes."

When I share this ideology with my mastermind, members often think "kids need discipline," or "there's only one way students learn." I agree that we need to keep everyone safe and show kids right from wrong. How about if we do it in a way that resonates with the individual instead of making school a place to chip away some of the best parts of a person's unique identity, and for no good purpose but to fit in to standardized measurements and scoring rubrics?

Force is **never** the answer. Motivation and inspiration will always supersede. Even the most interesting classroom subject will fall flat unless a person is motivated to learn it. Like I wrote in my first book: "Motivation precedes education." I found this fact astonishing when I looked back on my reading escapade at 18 years old. More on this journey later in the book but in short, I found myself with an insatiable hunger to read nonstop for nearly 2 years straight. I studied some of the most prolific entrepreneurs and investors. When I was in school, I couldn't even get through a chapter. What made the difference in my performance? My own motivation, when I wanted to read, it happened, when it was forced it didn't.

"Motivation precedes education."

That brings us to the most important question in your life: What are you motivated by? What lifts your spirits and has you whistling over your morning coffee? What energizes you and makes you smile?

Plug into that feeling, and you'll start becoming fully aligned and have the drive to:

1. Sustain through things that take time and effort.
2. Overcome tough times without quitting.
3. Never feel bored again.
4. Make money and have fun.

Make Money and Have Fun is not just some mantra or chant, it's a way of life. I haven't always been fully aligned, like everyone it took time to build a lifestyle by design. Many sleepless nights and early mornings were part of the journey. Today I am often referred to as a "Lifestyle Architect" or "Financial Fulfillment Expert" because of my ability to help others curate a particular lifestyle where they too can make money and have fun! This is why I started the "Make Money & Have Fun Mastermind". I wanted to bring together growth oriented, like minded individuals who are looking to create financial fulfillment in their life. The process is different for everyone, it's difficult, but absolutely worth it!

It's time to open your eyes to the opportunities all around, free yourself from the trappings of what you believe to be Everyday Life and, most importantly, make money and have fun!

If you believe it's your time and you're looking to surround yourself with others on the road to their best life head over to *makemoneyandhavefun.com/mastermind*

Chapter 2

BECOMING FULLY ALIGNED

I grew up living in Northeast Philadelphia. Like all kids, I had big dreams and aspirations, and I imagined myself going to exciting places and doing great things. Unfortunately, like I mentioned in the previous chapter, I didn't perform well in school, which dimmed the lights over what I believed I would be able to achieve. My mind became filled with limiting beliefs, negative thoughts and my dreams felt completely unattainable. I doubted my abilities, my self-worth, and assumed that my dreams just weren't meant for me.

To expand on my personal story from the last chapter, I was the kid who never fit in—the nerdy kid in the back of the room who never got the girl. I was ostracized, bullied and picked on. Other students avoided me because I was the weirdo, the oddball, the outcast.

Around third or fourth grade, I was diagnosed with ADHD. When the news came out, I was shocked. I felt damaged and alone, as if I was the only person in the world going through this struggle. It was a hard pill for me to swallow, both literally and figuratively.

At the time I felt like I had no choice but to press on with this new label that made me feel branded as a freak. Depressed and overwhelmed, I continued through grade school until graduating eighth grade in 2009. Throughout that summer, I told myself, "When I enter high school, I want to become someone new!" This was the theme for my entire summer.

Inside me, a silent voice whispered that it didn't matter what I did. It didn't matter how I did it. All that really mattered was who I became. Honestly, I was fed up at this point, I couldn't stand it anymore. I had enough of the rejection, the shaming, the mental and verbal abuse had finally taken its toll. I had read in one of the books on my reading escapade "Change happens when the pain of same is greater than the pain of change." I followed this advice and chose to use my pain as motivation to propel me forward. The realization that I had more to give, and I was worth more is what allowed me to embrace this change. Ultimately, I had decided that enough is enough and I took a stand.

"All that really mattered was who I became."

My first step in becoming someone new was accepting who I already was. So, I said: "I'm Fred Posimo, the kid with ADHD who doesn't like sports and can't name the top five trending songs on Spotify this week. I'm the kid who pursued a different path, the kid who went against the grain."

I no longer viewed my situation as a negative, I turned my obstacle into an opportunity. I realized I was completely and totally in control of my life. My potential as a human hadn't been fulfilled yet, my dreams and aspirations were not yet a reality. By regaining control of my own personal power, I was taking the first step in making a lasting change for myself. This led to three Catalyst Moments in my life.

> "I no longer viewed my situation as a negative,
> I turned my obstacle into an opportunity."

Catalyst Moment #1

In high school, I showed appreciation and respect to every soul I came across in those hallways. Granted, I didn't have many "friends," but I did have acquaintances and strong relationships. Some of them developed after only a few minutes. Every time I shared a handshake and a smile, I knew I was on the right path. I already felt changes taking root during freshman year. My confidence was up, my communication skills seemed to increase, and I generally found myself displaying less social awkwardness then what I had grown familiar with in grade school. Freshman & Sophomore year I basically found a comfort I didn't know could exist within a school. Granted my academics stayed generally the same and I still felt like a square peg in a round hole, only now it was as if I figured out how to navigate the sea of round pegs I was surrounded by. For once I didn't feel so out of place, identification of my problem turned out to be the first step towards solution!

Then, in my junior year, I took a class entitled Entrepreneurship. When I signed up, I had no idea what that word meant. I only knew that it was a business course because the previous year the course name was General Business. From the first class, I was undoubtedly and irrevocably in love with this class and with the idea of entrepreneurship. My entire world changed, and I couldn't wait until the next class.

> "Identification of my problem
> turned out to be the first step towards solution!"

No one was more surprised than me. My grade-school self could never love any course in any school anywhere. However, I was no longer the same person. In many ways, I left eighth grade a boy and entered high school a man with 100 percent control over my destiny. It's funny to think all it took was making a decision and sticking to it. The summer after eighth grade could be considered the straw that broke the camel's back. I was fed up with myself and who I was, frankly, I even hated myself at times! That's when I made a decision and committed to it, I was going to change myself no matter what it took.

In Entrepreneurship class, the teacher oftentimes put the regular course curriculum on hold to focus on real-world skills and opportunities. For instance, he would teach us about subjects like financial literacy, Real Estate investing and much, much, much more.

He would open the class to discussion, and we would talk about the stock market or investing or other topics. I loved it, and I was fully engaged. For the first time, a teacher left the traditional Round Peg format and opened the class to discussion, exploration and basically, Square Peg thinking.

I remember one day in particular when the teacher explained the concept of Real Estate investing. The memory is still so vivid in my head, he used a blue marker on the white board to draw the houses and run the numbers demonstrating how to make money ("cashflow" a term I didn't learn until later) from a rental property. As a seventeen-year-old, I had never previously fathomed such an idea. After he finished the demonstration, the floodgates of my mind opened to a plethora of possibilities and opportunities that never existed before.

> "I felt as if the floodgates of my mind opened."

I couldn't get enough. That class changed the trajectory of my entire life from feeling lost to goal-oriented. Prior to this I had no clue what to do with my future and frankly I was a little scared. There were no jobs that seemed to interest me no matter how hard I looked. Now for the first time, I realized there were other paths aside from just the job paths. This was my first catalyst moment.

Catalyst Moment #2

When I was 7 years old, I began studying Martial Arts. By the time I was seventeen, I had earned my second-degree blackbelt, and felt I had more to offer than just attending two 45-minute classes per week. So, I began volunteering as an instructor every night after school. Initially, I made no money, but I loved every second of it. I continued volunteering after high school and soon was on payroll as an instructor for another five years. I attribute part of my transformation after eighth grade to my martial arts training. Martial arts is really personal development shrouded by kicks and punches. So in essence I had a mindset "forged by fire" since I was seven years old.

Shortly before my eighteenth birthday, a coworker at the karate school told me he would loan me a book as a birthday gift. I was grateful for the kind gesture but terrified at the same time. I had never in my life read an entire book from cover to cover. When I received it, I felt like it was the most overwhelming chore I had ever been asked to do, but I braced myself and accepted *The Total Money Makeover* by Dave Ramsey.

"I had never in my life read an entire book from cover to cover."

Looking closer, I noticed this book was different from what I was used to. My upbringing in Catholic school showcased many fiction books, and I knew about the fiction section in Barnes and Noble. I also knew behind their massive fiction section was a small area called Self-help, but reading one of those books had never crossed my mind. Something inside me winced at the very idea.

When I got home, I placed the book on my nightstand, and I paced back and forth. I needed to justify in my head why I should read this book—it seemed like an insurmountable chore. No, worse. To me, 220 pages felt like climbing Mount Everest... twice... in the dead of winter. "No way can I do this," I said to myself. Yet, at the same time I felt an intense obligation because I received such a thoughtful gesture from a friend.

I thought he had loaned it to me, which added to my already high stress. "Great, not only do I have to read this book, but I need to do it in a time crunch as well" I thought to myself.

This was going to be a long night.

A few minutes later, I decided to get some sleep before I began this frightening task. I woke up the next morning, and I stared at the book on my nightstand. Dave Ramsey's face on the cover stared back at me with his stupid smile. In my head, the metaphor shifted, and I was no longer facing a killer mountain but a beast wanting a fight. I felt as if I were stepping into a ring, preparing to take a ferocious punch.

> "I felt as if I were stepping into a ring,
> preparing to take a ferocious punch."

I grabbed the book, opened it up, read the first page, got distracted, put it down and forgot about it.

Over the next several days, I'd pick the book up, read a few pages and put it down, pick the book up, read a few pages, put it down. I'd forget what page I was on, start over, pick the book up, read a few pages, and put it down.

Two weeks passed before I realized I had to snap myself out of this. I looked at myself in the mirror and had a transformative moment, similar to the summer after eighth grade when I decided to change my entire identity. But this time, I would make the change in an hour instead of all summer.

I looked at myself in the mirror and said, "Get it together! What's wrong with you? You've done so many hard things and accomplished so much in your life. You graduated from high school. You have a second-degree black belt, and you can't read a dang book? Sit down and read it!"

That's exactly what I did. I sat down. I opened the book, and I read it. I did the same thing the next day and the next day and the next day and the next day. Thirty days later, I closed the back cover. My mind was racing. I could barely lift my head. After reading that book, it was as if everything I thought I knew about this world was wrong, but I couldn't quite put my finger on what was right or how to find it. At that moment it was if I had the opportunity to look behind the proverbial "curtain of life," but only for a brief second. I said to myself, "I know there's something else out there. I don't know what it is, but I need to find out." This was the second catalyst moment in my life.

> "I know there's something else out there,
> I don't know what it is, but I need to find out."

Suddenly, I was on a mission to uncover everything I could learn. I told myself, "It took me thirty days to read that book, so I'm going to read a book a month for 12 months. I'll read 12 books a year."

I stayed true to my mission. Over the next 12 months, I picked up some of the most popular titles in all of self-help history: *Think and Grow Rich, Rich Dad, Poor Dad, How to Win Friends and Influence People, The 10X Rule*, and many more. I devoured books on financial literacy, human behavior, psychology, relationships, success, you name it. I gave myself a Barnes and Noble education on personal development.

By the end of the year, I had surpassed my goal, and I read 16 books! I exceeded my own expectations, but most importantly, I had uncovered a whole new world—that world that I knew existed, but I wasn't sure where to find it. Later, that idea would develop into what I now describe as "The 2 Worlds" (more on this in the next chapter).

"I had uncovered a whole new world."

About four or five books into my reading marathon, I recognized a pattern amongst all these personal development books. I said to myself, "Why don't I take concepts and pieces from each of these books that I've read and compile them into my own book?" That idea stuck in my brain and became something I wanted for two reasons: One, because I believed I had something to say, and two, because I needed to prove to myself that I could do it.

From the time I was 19 until I was 21, I wrote. I wrote inconsistently. I wrote sporadically. I wrote horribly. I couldn't stick to a schedule or meet a writing goal, but at 21 years old I published my first book: *The [R]evolutionary Mindset*. It is on Amazon, and it is mine, you can pick up a copy at fredposimo.com.

It's an achievement, and I'm proud of it, but it was merely a steppingstone. I wasn't focused on selling it, but I loved telling people about it and sharing it with others.

"At 21 years old I published my first book."

After that, my life stagnated a bit. I was now a full-time, paid martial arts instructor, teaching karate six or seven days a week, often multiple times a day. I was training at multiple locations, in multiple styles and growing myself as a martial artist. Eventually, I reached a point where martial arts became a burden. It was almost like eating too much ice cream. I loved it, but I needed a change.

With no college education, I was unsure how to pursue the job world in corporate America. I had never been on a job interview, and it was intimidating. Since I was unfamiliar with how the system worked, I went for low-hanging fruit. I talked to my brother-in-law who got me a job as a leasing agent at PMC Property Group.

I hated that job starting on Day One. Actually, the job wasn't bad. I should say, I hated the environment. I hated having to clock in every day at 9:00 AM and clock out at 5:00 PM. I had to scan my fingerprint and enter a code to get in and out of work every day. I hated wearing a uniform every day, having to dress a certain way and look a certain way. I hated the monotony, the day-by-day drudgery, going through the same script, seeing the same people, entering the same building, saying the same things, sitting behind the same computer screen. It was nauseating.

About six months in, while scanning my fingerprint to clock in I realized, *They don't even do this to prisoners!* It was time for me to leave.

Of all the books I read, one that stood out to me was *Rich Dad, Poor Dad*. It re-ignited the flame I had discovered years ago in entrepreneurship class. Since before leaving the dojo, I knew I wanted to enter the Real Estate investing world—it lit me up when I learned about it in high school, and it lit me up when I read about it in books. I was never cut out for a job and "passive income" through real estate seemed like the way to go.

I remembered one of my adult students at the karate school telling me about a Real Estate investor in Philadelphia who led a community of investors. They came together to learn and grow as business owners and entrepreneurs. When I first heard about it, I wanted to go to the meetings, but my work hours conflicted with their meeting time. With the job change, I no longer had a conflict. I called the guy to see if those meetings were still available. He told me to come by.

"Passive Income through Real Estate seemed like the way to go."

Catalyst Moment #3

In April of 2017, I found a community of like-minded people who were Square Pegs like me. They told stories about how they were outcasts and oddballs and weirdos in school. They read self-help books in their basements or watched educational YouTube videos instead of staying up and watching Netflix or writing posts on Twitter or watching the Super Bowl. Finally, I found people who got me, and I got them. Time and time again I heard the phrase: "your network is your net worth." It's essentially a cliché in the personal development world. The profundity of this phrase really didn't sink in until I changed my environment and started hanging around new people. Put another way, "you are the sum of your 5 closest friends." I like to change that phrase to "If you have 4 broke friends you're the fifth." Conversely "if you have 4 rich friends you're the fifth." So, the question is, what kind of friends do you want to be around? After fully understanding the power of associations I decided to create my own, that's what *"The Make Money & Have Fun Mastermind"* is all about. It's a group of goal oriented like-minded individuals who are looking to create financial fulfillment together. You can learn more at makemoneyandhavefun.com/mastermind

"I found a community of like-minded people
who were Square Pegs like me."

This was the first time I paid serious money for an education in Real Estate investing. Prior to this point, I had tried to do everything for free or almost free. This is when I realized that paying a high price tag makes the road to success much, much shorter than trying to find your own way for free. If you want to get somewhere fast, pay for education and surround yourself with successful people. Those who invest the most in themselves will have the most invested back into them.

"Those who invest the most in themselves
will have the most invested back into them."

I started attending meetings every single Thursday. I was there day in and day out, learning, absorbing, growing, changing and becoming a new person. In a short year, I learned an astronomical amount about Real Estate Investing. I never could have achieved this by myself. My community helped pull me in the right direction.

This community put me in touch with some of the biggest names in the industry. I sat kneecap to kneecap with multi-millionaires. I got the phone numbers of extraordinarily successful business owners and had private one-on-one calls with them about ways to change my life and grow, to become the person that I've wanted to be. This was jet engine propulsion. Today I lead *"The Make Money & Have Fun Mastermind"* as a way of simulating the same experience I've had for others and to open my rolodex of successful individuals to the members.

Up until this point, I felt my dreams were far away from financial fulfillment. With a few small moves and a few big decisions, I landed where I wanted to be in my early 20's.

At 23 years old, I purchased my first investment property. It was, without a doubt, the scariest, riskiest, biggest decision I had ever made in my life. By the same token, it was, without a doubt, the greatest and best decision I ever made in my life.

"At 23 years old, I purchased my first investment property."

I did much of the deal with none of my own money, using strategies that I had learned from my nine months in this community. I did a lot of stuff right. I did a lot of stuff wrong. But the fact remains, I continued to grow.

Six months later, I bought my second property, a four-unit apartment building right around the corner from the first property. This has been my favorite asset thus far, but it has also been a long and winding road. A lot of dark, scary nights happened in that building where I thought I would have no heat in the building and nights where I had to go to court and face lawsuits. I went through ups and downs, lefts and rights, failures and successes.

I learned, at the end of the day, what you do last is what counts. When you're engaged in something that energizes you, even if most people would give up, you keep on going. Throughout all my trials and tribulations, there was one prevailing thought which kept me alive: "This is the point where "most people" would give up... and I never wanted to be "most people.""

"This is the point where "most people" would give up...
and I never wanted to be "most people."

So, that brings me to this question: Who do you want to be?

Chapter 3

FREE YOUR MIND

I f you've never watched *The Matrix*, stop and watch it before reading another word. The first time I saw it, I was seven years old, and the experience resonated with me on so many levels that I never forgot it. As a young adult, I watched it again, and the truth hit me like a ton of bricks. I understood so much more, as if I were seeing it again for the first time. The story is both compelling and scary, not because it's a horror film but because of the truth within it. The Matrix is my favorite movie of all time.

"You've been living in a dream world."

In the movie, this chilling statement by the great Morpheus to the young and somewhat naive Neo sends chills through the viewers. At this moment, you feel Neo's total confusion as his foundations melt away and, most of all, his consuming curiosity to know more overtakes him. This notion is as true in real life as it is in the movie. I am Neo, and so are you.

On this planet, you wake up every day in pursuit of something. Often, you have no idea what you're searching for, yet you love the search itself. The certainty of uncertainty makes you feel alive.

"The certainty of uncertainty makes you feel alive."

Have you ever felt like something bigger is out there, like we're all pawns on a chessboard, trying desperately to understand and interact with the hands that move us? Have you ever felt confined to the will of those hands, as though your life is not of your own choice but rather dictated by something bigger?

"You're probably feeling a bit like Alice, tumbling down the rabbit hole."

This is how Morpheus described it to Neo.

If you're feeling like Neo at the beginning of that movie, you are absolutely and 100 percent correct. Bigger forces are at play. Here's the best part: not only are you correct, but you're also on the right path. Your life doesn't have to be out of your control forever.

"Follow the white rabbit."

Like Neo, at first your life appears robotic and mundane, filled with drudgery and boredom. "Same stuff, different day," is your mantra. Over the years, you become numb to it.

You believe that's all there is to life because you listen to incorrect and flat-out stupid advice. No more, America!

It's time someone came by to splash you in the face with ice cold water and wake you up. My hope is this book will be that for you.

What separated Neo from almost everyone else—he never stopped searching. Well into his adult years he continued to believe something else was out there. He followed the white rabbit. When he discovered Wonderland, he also found the tools to break free from the bondage he'd been living in.

"Like a splinter in your mind."

All right, let me stop with all the ethereal stuff and get to the point.

If you're miserable, fed up or frustrated with your life, you most likely feel that way because you have been duped into thinking you need to live a certain way. You've been living in a matrix, so to speak, where your decisions were predetermined before you made them. You had an illusion that you were in control, but, in reality, you were not.

"You are a slave, like everyone else, born into bondage."

In my first book, *The {R}evolutionary Mindset,* my favorite chapter is entitled, "Slaves of the System." Since writing that chapter, this phrase has followed me everywhere. Basically, it sums up the idea that none of us are free in this world. We're all slaves to the systems around us—the government system, the banking system, the corporate system, the medical system, and on and on.

Red Pill or Blue Pill?

In *The Matrix*, Morpheus had one shot, a sales pitch to convince Neo that he could break free. I'm here for the same reason. This book is your guide to breaking out of the Round Peg matrix and radically embracing your Square Peg life. Not only will you break free to live your authentic best life, but you will help others as well. Follow me down this rabbit hole.

> "I'll show you how deep the rabbit hole goes."

I'm not going to lie. This journey is scary, controversial and world-changing, but it's going to be worth it. You'll leave behind the false structures that make up your life. Pre-conceived notions, dogmas, mantras and stigmas will be part of your past. You will become the fully aligned person you're capable of being.

At a seminar I attended, I heard Tony Robbins say that Jim Rohn once told him: "Become a millionaire not for the million dollars, but for what it will make of you to achieve it." Take a leap of faith, and no matter how contradictory things might seem, keep going. Do it for who you will become. This is the journey I've been embarking upon since the summer after eighth grade. Deep down, I believe each of us have the same goal: to make each day better than our last. In the past half decade or so I have seen immense change in my personal and financial life, yet I am still on this journey. Destinations are fleeting but journeys can last forever. I continue to pursue daily growth, and I encourage you to tag along with me.

If you decide to stop here, imagine taking the blue pill. The story ends, you wake up in your bed tomorrow and believe whatever you want to believe. But if you keep going, imagine taking the red pill. The story continues, and I will show you how deep the rabbit hole goes.

"Remember all I offer is the truth, nothing more."

The Visible World vs. The Invisible World

Humanity is divided into two worlds as mentioned in the previous chapter. While we all inhabit planet earth, our perceptions of the world fall into two categories: the visible and the invisible. The visible world consists of self-imposed manmade systems. We see these in the philosophies and dogmas, the mantras and ideologies man has put together over the eons of our human history.

"The world has been pulled over your eyes to blind you from the truth."

The visible world is a structured, systematic and robotic way of life. This is the world others want us to see—the advertisements, media, culture, pop culture, status and *status quo*. In many ways this world consists of emotions and feelings that put people on autopilot.

The visible world is like a stage show. We get our tickets, sit in our seats and watch the visible world play out. Based on what we see on the stage, we get a feeling for what we believe to be true and false, the mythology behind the performance.

This world appears orderly and expected. It portrays life as a timeline—grade school, high school, part-time job, college, full-time job, apartment, car, spouse, house, children, retirement, decline and death. We quantify and qualify ourselves by where we are on that timeline. How do we measure up with where we are supposed to be? Are we far enough along for our age? Or maybe we pride ourselves for being ahead and retiring early. No matter what the individual details are, we see everyone as having the same life, played out as different variations on one theme. I feel like my entire life I've been pulled away from this world and toward the invisible world but never had the capacity to realize it. Therefore, I fought it for a while until I realized I was meant to be somewhere else. I'm not meant for the "visible world" and like most, that made me angry and frustrated at first. When I realized that I wasn't "flawed," everything changed. Sometimes the answer has nothing to do with changing you, it may just be as simple as changing your environment.

> "You are here because you know something,
> what you know you can't explain."

The invisible world is not seen but discovered. When we pull back the curtain, we look beyond the myths to find truth. This is what I glimpsed at when I read *"The Total Money Makeover"* during my second catalyst moment. The invisible world means creating your life on your own terms in a celebration of creativity and non-conformity. The curtain lifts away and from our vantage point backstage, we have a clear view of the set, the props, the characters and the audience that make up the show of our lives. We are bold enough to take a good look and hold steady without looking away. We are the inventors, innovators, entrepreneurs, investors and meditators.

"Nobody can be told what the matrix is, you have to see it for yourself."

This world is not for the fainthearted. Some take a peek and quickly drop the curtain. Reality can be messy. Most people shy away from the mirrors in this world because of their stark honesty. The only way to remain in this invisible world is by consistently digging out from under our embedded philosophies and dogmas. This work isn't done in a day, and it can be very uncomfortable. Staying in the invisible world means living with the discomfort.

One world cannot exist without the other. Without the work behind the scenes, the show could not go on. We cannot see the full picture without acknowledging both of them.

Like Morpheus, who held out his two hands with the red pill and blue pill, my intent is simply to show you the options. In this lightning-fast technology storm and all the opportunities it offers, understanding our options has become more and more pressing. Once we realize that our limits are merely illusions on the stage, we can head toward our full potential and never stop moving forward.

So, what will it be? Red pill or blue?

Chapter 4

THE QUESTION QUEST

et's slow down for a moment, at this point you're likely asking yourself – "Why are we talking about mindset?" "I Just want to learn how to make money and have fun." I'm so glad you asked! The answer is, without first developing the proper mindset I cannot teach you about money, fun, fulfillment, or frankly anything. Even if I shared the most groundbreaking financial strategies with you right now, they would in essence "fall on deaf ears" or, in this case, "a deaf brain." These chapters are necessary to prepare you to fully absorb the coming information on how to make money and have fun. This reminds me of the old Zen proverb:

A student goes to visit a famous Zen master. While the master quietly served tea, the student talked about Zen. The master poured the visitor's cup to the brim, and then kept pouring. The student watched the overflowing cup until he could no longer restrain him-

self. *"It's full! No more will go in!"* the student blurted. *"This is you,"* the master replied, *"Like this cup so too is your mind full. How can I show you Zen unless you first empty your cup?"*

Speaking of mindset, let's go back to the above-mentioned question "Why are we talking about mindset?" I truly meant it when I said, "I'm so glad you asked." I have found that most people underestimate the power and use of asking questions. In fact, I firmly believe more people should ask questions more often. Beware of the "coaches" or "mentors' who are quick to give feedback and slow to ask questions.

> "Beware of the "coaches" or "mentors" who are quick
> to give feedback and slow to ask questions."

If you've ever been coached by me 1 on 1 or during my mastermind you'll know that I'll often spend 10 to 15 minutes asking questions before ever offering a peep of feedback. This will often times frustrate students until they realize the power. Questions create clarity and the more clarity we can create the better we can serve others and ourselves. Did you ever notice prior to reading the chapter title that the beginning of the word Question is Quest? I don't believe this was an accident because in many ways asking questions takes us on mental quests, asking a better question is like being handed a map to better navigate our quest. Even more powerful than asking questions of others is asking questions of yourself through thought. Thought is simply the process of asking and answering questions.

"Thought is simply the process of asking and answering questions."

When we ask ourselves questions, our brain immediately tracks down answers. The types of questions we ask will often directly affect our immediate mood. Some questions are positive, and some are negative. Some lift us up while others bring us down. I want to use this chapter to step away from the ethereal and into the practical. On that note, let's do an exercise.

You might ask, "How can I ask better questions?" Asking this question, shows you are already on the right track.

"How am I on the right track?" you might ask.

The answer: How is How!

Huh?

"How is How!"

By asking yourself questions beginning with *How* you inspire action and receive tremendous amounts of clarity.

Think of a time when you had to make an emotionally difficult decision. I'm willing to bet you asked yourself a ton of questions during that process. Let's use deciding to quit your job as an example. You made the decision. Now the questions begin pouring in.

"How should I approach this?"

"How can I find the best time?"

"How should I word my resignation?"

"How much notice do I give?"

These "How" questions create clarity and allow you to develop a solid strategy.

Unfortunately, many times our inner dialogue sounds more like this:

"Is this really the right decision?"

"What will my friends and coworkers think?"

"What if the conversation ends in disaster?"

"What if my boss doesn't like me anymore?"

"What if they don't recommend me for other jobs?"

Notice how these questions—the way they are phrased—disempower you. They bury you in an emotional low and influence your decision making in a more negative way.

In my studies, I recognized that many of the most successful people on this planet use the power of questions to their advantage, this is your opportunity to do the same. Let's start with the granddaddy of all thing's personal development: Tony Robbins. He explains how our brains are servomechanisms, meaning they hunt down answers like a heat-seeking missile.

The key is to stop asking yourself limiting questions and ask yourself empowering questions instead. Like the old adage says, "What we focus on we get more of."

In order to change the quality of your questions you need to pay attention to where your focus is. In the "quitting your job" scenario above, you can choose to focus on the stress of breaking that connection, or you can focus on the opportunity of starting fresh. It is the same event, yet your focus results in vastly different feelings, emotions and subsequently - actions. All feelings stem from your questions, not your answers.

"All feelings stem from our questions, not your answers."

Another fabulous book I read was titled, *QBQ! The Question Behind the Question* by John Miller. This fantastic, quick read says a QBQ is:

1. A question beginning with What or How, not why, when or who.
2. A question containing I, not they, we or you.
3. A question focusing on action.

For example: "How am I going to approach my boss to announce my resignation?"

This question starts with how, contains I, and the action is "approaching." This is a QBQ!

Asking QBQs energizes your thoughts and feelings. They help you build personal accountability and avoid victim mentalities, complaining and procrastination.

Your goal is to eliminate what John Miller calls IQs (Incorrect Questions) and replace them with self-accountable QBQs.

If you are thinking, "How can I do that?" you are following along brilliantly. This question starts with how, contains "I", and the action is to do. This is a QBQ. The answer to your question is the last piece of the puzzle.

"How can I do that?"

In *Rich Dad Poor Dad* by Robert Kiyosaki, one of his most profound ideas was the paradigm shift from "I can't…" to "How can I...?" Although his book is classified as financial literacy, I like to think of it as financial psychology because it teaches so much about mindset and thought patterns much like the first section of this book.

In his discussion about the different perspectives between average people and rich people, Kiyosaki says that average people think, "I can't afford that," whereas rich people think, "How can I afford that?" We can create abundance in our lives if we simply choose to switch our thought process from "I can't" to "How can I?" which, by the way, is a QBQ.

Questions are the gateway to creating financial fulfillment in your life. To become fully aligned, we must begin asking better questions. When you do, you will open the door to a new perspective and a new mindset. If you want to become a millionaire, ask the same questions millionaires ask. When you ask the same questions millionaires ask, your mindset will start to change. If you want to start making more money and having more fun, you guessed it, ask the right questions.

"Questions are the gateway to creating financial fulfillment in your life."

All that said, there's only one question that truly matters... Yours!

Here's a fun exercise:

Think of common questions you've been asking yourself lately and write them down in the left column. In the right column replace the question with its more empowering "QBQ Counterpart" then implement the new questions and see the results for yourself:

Common Question	New QBQ
_____	_____
_____	_____
_____	_____
_____	_____
_____	_____
_____	_____
_____	_____
_____	_____
_____	_____
_____	_____
_____	_____
_____	_____
_____	_____
_____	_____
_____	_____
_____	_____
_____	_____

Chapter 5

LIFESTYLE BY DESIGN

O ne of my business partners recently described me as a "Lifestyle Architect" at first I laughed, then I realized he might be on to something. Make money and have fun is more than just financial literacy and finding your why. It's about designing your own lifestyle, creating an environment you never want to retire from. The goal is to find "your thing" that lights you up so much that you never want to leave! Everything we have discussed so far has been building up to this chapter. When we embrace being a square peg, free our mind, and ask better questions we begin bridging the gap between our passion and prosperity so we can become our own lifestyle architect! It's time for us to say "no" to status quo and grow beyond what "they" say success looks like.

After writing my first book I realized that mindset is the foundation. It is the starting point, the ground floor upon which all of life is built upon. When we can learn to control and better yet curate our mindset, it's as if everything else will begin to fall into place. I always recommend mindset as the first step, but we must grow beyond there. Look around and you'll notice that mindset is the great differentiator. The only distinction between average sports enthusiasts and Olympians is mindset, between average people who make a donation once in a while and philanthropists is mindset, between average income earners and millionaires is mindset. If you no longer want average results, stop thinking with an average mind. Mindset is the single difference between our current state and attaining success, whatever success looks like to you. It's time for us to level up our mindset!

As we learned in the last chapter, questions are the answer. In order to break out of our current mindset we must begin to question the *status quo* . The world is filled with foundational beliefs. Society conditions us to think, act and live in certain ways. We accept these ideas without questioning, yet many of them are not actually true or only partially true. Often, we hear things and without question take them as fact and begin implementing these new ideas. Although I applaud you for taking action this is typically more detrimental than beneficial. For instance, saving money: saving money is a great practice but when and how we save is just as important as saving money. Unfortunately, what usually happens is you hear a friend. Co-worker, or loved one tell you "you need to save money" and without questioning how or when you just start doing what you think that means. I did the same thing at first. Stockpiled as much money in the bank as I could until I started an intense study of money in my late teens and early 20's, what I discovered is that "you need to save money" is true but only a half-truth. Wealthy people save their money, but not the way most of us do. (We'll discuss this in more depth in the next section.)

What I want to do now is go through many of the perpetuated mantras, dogmas, beliefs and philosophies many of us subscribe to and expose the half-truth behind.

Let's play a game, Truth or Half-Truth?

Reading Books Makes You Smarter.

I have heard my whole life, "You need to read books if you want to be smarter." This statement represents all-or-nothing thinking: If reading is good, then not reading is bad.

While I do agree that you can learn much from reading, this statement leaves out an important element. Reading the right books will make you smarter, books that focus on growth, books that teach, books that expand your thinking. Reading for entertainment doesn't provide the same benefits as reading books of substance. After reading that first book, like I mentioned in the previous chapters, I instantly became a voracious reader. As I went through each book, I literally felt my growth happening in front of me. I went from being anxious and fearful of reading to literally feeling my mind expand and my belief systems began to shift just by reading the right books.

"Reading the *right* books will make you smarter."

Knowledge is Power.

You've probably heard the phrase "Knowledge is power." Truth is, knowledge is not power. Knowledge is knowledge. How many people do you know who are knowledgeable yet still powerless? Knowledge is like a bullet. By itself it's useless. It needs a gun to create power. The "gun" for knowledge is application. Application of knowledge is power.

"Knowing is not enough, we must apply."
~Bruce Lee

Application is perhaps the most crucial element for creating power. After all, knowledge without application is as useless as no knowledge at all. It's easy to collect facts and philosophies. The challenging part is applying them to everyday life and moving in the right direction. I would change the statement to: Applied knowledge is power.

Reading this book could be a passive experience where you merely read the words on the page and decide that they resonate with you or not. You could also use this book to have an active experience by using the knowledge contained here and taking action on it through journaling, mapping out strategies, setting and attaining goals, making and applying decisions to shift habits and mindset, etc. The power is in the application. Like my good friend Dr. Greg Reid says: "It's the "Action" in the law of attr<u>action</u> that makes your dreams come true."

"Applied knowledge is power."

Time Management = Success.

Motivational speakers often say, "If you want to be successful learn how to manage your time." This buzz phrase has become so immersed in society that people blindly follow it without fully understanding what it means. Feeling too busy is never about a lack of time but rather a lack of priorities .

As you know, a day has twenty-four hours. Some of us power through those twenty-four hours and make massive progress. Others consistently get lost in a crazed whirlwind of angst and begin making statements like, "I don't have enough time," "I am too busy," or "I can't do that now!" To them, time is the culprit. This is delusional thinking, out of focus and off balance.

Instead, shift your paradigm. Priorities are the culprit, not time.

"Priorities are the culprit, not time."

Barring cataclysmic disruptions, you know your days entail eating, sleeping, using the restroom, work, rest and socializing. When you are fully aligned in your purpose, you pick up speed through those twenty-four hours and get more done. Instead of wasting time why not invest your time by purposefully planning your day. Do not waste, Invest!

By intentionally mapping out your day, you can create more efficiency in your life. Intention is nothing more than the purposeful application of energy. Take the time to give your day purpose and watch this carry through the weeks, months and years to ultimately create your destiny.

"Intention is the purposeful application of energy."

No one controls time. What we can control is our priorities. Being fully aligned is also about having your priorities in order.

We can literally feel the difference, the times you blaze through your tasks are times of full alignment, begin to analyze those moments, recognize them and look for more!

I'd rather focus on priority management instead of time management. Priority management, in my opinion, should become the modern buzz phrase of society. The saying should go: "If you want to be successful, learn how to manage your priorities."

"If you want to be successful learn how to manage your priorities."

Learn to Multitask.

Multi-tasking is probably one of the most perpetuated myths out there today. We throw the word around like it's nothing. What's even worse is that others get mad at us when we're not multi-tasking. Building businesses in my early twenties I learned firsthand that there is no such thing as multi-tasking. In fact, I almost had everything blow up in my face because of this. Around the age of 25 I started about 6 different businesses simultaneously, an investing business, a training company, a coaching business, a branding business, a credit repair business etc. Guess what happened? That's right, they all failed within months, it wasn't until I got rid of everything except for my mastermind that I truly started to see success, and very quickly also!

We often hear speakers pontificate about how "rich people have multiple streams of income." This is true but the method through which they got there is not always what we think. Creating multiple streams of income or businesses or even tasks does not mean to wake up in the morning and work on all 7 different things. The game is to build them one at a time, not all at once. We can create as many businesses, incomes, or tasks as we want, but we need to focus on one at a time. The best I ever heard this said was by my good friend Dr. Obom Bowen, he said "If you're trying to work on 7 things at once you are really only working on one and have 6 distractions."

Some gurus teach that splitting your focus helps to increase productivity. I beg to differ. This phrasing is misleading. A more appropriate phrase would be to divide your focus.

Think of it this way, splitting your focus would be like trying to read the left page of this book with your left eye while simultaneously reading the right page with your right eye. Uhhh... not so easy.

Splitting your focus is like unraveling a rope on one end to form a Y. If your focus is split into two opposing directions, neither side receives as much focus as the initial rope. Instead, divide your focus. Focus on one thing at one time to ensure maximum efficiency.

"Focus on one thing at one time to ensure maximum efficiency."

Focus is the key, and we can only focus on one thing at one time. Instead of trying to multi-task pick one thing. Your one thing that really moves you, the thing you feel fully aligned with and double down on that. Keep everything else as an idea until this one thing takes off and becomes self-sustaining, then go to the next thing. Even right now as I write this, I have multiple businesses in my head that I will create one day, but right now they're not my focus, that's why they're in my head and not being mentioned. Start doing the same with your business, focus, double down, and eliminate all your distractions, you'll literally feel the difference!

When you step back and take the time to think, myths will show up all around you. Take a look at your world with fresh eyes and begin questioning everything like we mentioned in the last chapter. What other half-truths can you find? It's time to regain control, fully align yourself with your soul purpose and begin living the life you were meant to live!

Chapter 6

THE 5 PILLARS OF LIFE

Before we move into the next section it is imperative that you first learn this principle. Throughout my research I came to the realization that life is made up of 5 basic parts, or what I like to call pillars.

The 5 Pillars are:
1. Physical
2. Mental
3. Emotional
4. Spiritual
5. Financial

I will explain why I use the word pillars in the next paragraph but first you need to understand that these 5 pieces represent one singular whole and without even one of them everything would fall off balance, this brings me to the "pillars" analogy.

Imagine planet earth is no longer suspended by gravity, but instead it is held up by 5 pillars. That means these pillars are non-negotiable and permanent. If you try to bend or break them, your world as you know it will fall. You cannot avoid, circumvent, remove, or destroy any of them, like I mentioned before, these 5 pillars represent one whole which must not be disrupted. Many will try to fight against one of them, and it's almost always the financial pillar. People who resist addressing the financial pillar often make statements like:

"There's more to life than money."
"The money doesn't matter."
"I'm here to be of service, not make money."

No matter how much you push back or retaliate against money, money still permeates life. You must have it to exist. I base this justification on the American economic system I grew up in. Here we live in an economy based on transactional commerce through the medium which we call "money." However transactional commerce has permeated life even before the invention of the fungible medium known as the U.S. Dollar. We'll go into more detail in the next section, but just remember that anytime you are creating a value-based transaction you are engaging the financial pillar of your life. The same concept is true for the other pillars as well. Ignore them at your own peril.

Each of the pillars has its own characteristics, its own advantages and its own challenges. Fully understanding the 5 Pillars and how they rank up in your life will help you narrow down your genuine passions and purpose.

As you read through the descriptions of each pillar, begin to ask yourself how important that pillar is to you personally right now. Rank each one on a scale from 1-10, 1 being not at all important and 10 being the driving force in your habits and lifestyle. Remember to be honest with yourself as you go through.

Physical Pillar

The physical pillar encompasses several areas of life, including health, fitness, personal appearance and your style. In rating the physical pillar, ask how much time, effort and focus you direct toward your physical body. Do you belong to a gym or other fitness organization? Are you concerned about healthy food or follow a diet regimen? Do you spend time selecting clothing, whether you are shopping or dressing for an outing? Do you have a consistent grooming routine? Do you follow celebrities in areas of fitness or style?

Someone who rates their physical pillar as a 10 out of 10 in importance would have a tight physique, immaculate grooming and consistently show their unique style. They choose to invest in their physical appearance before allotting time and resources to other activities. They consistently put their physical pillar first.

If you rank high on the physical pillar, you probably:

- Belong to a gym or other fitness organization
- Maintain a healthy diet focused on low calories with high nutrition and balanced energy

- Have a personal grooming routine and maintain a wardrobe of carefully chosen clothes and accessories for a variety of occasions
- Are Always aware of your personal numbers: weight, workout stats, body measurements, body-mass index, etc.

Role Models: Jet Li, Arnold Schwarzenegger, David Beckham

Mental Pillar

Developing and expanding the mind are important components of the mental pillar. Education is definitely important to you if you rank your mental pillar high. You study different schools of thought and follow thought gurus. You devour the latest books and talk about new concepts with the same enthusiasm as a sports enthusiast discussing their favorite team.

Someone who rates their mental pillar as a 10 out of 10 would be an education junkie who papers the office wall with certifications, degrees and awards. You spend your savings on classes and might neglect your relationships when delving into a new topic or perspective. You might get stuck toying with concepts rather than taking action to put those concepts into practice in the real world. You are an educator or philosopher who lives primarily in the world of ideas.

If you rank high on the mental pillar, you probably:

- Have an organized schedule
- Belong to book clubs and attend seminars
- Always learn something new and inform others of facts

- Implement systems for your home, family, career and hobbies
- Value integrity and truth
- Sometimes fall into analysis paralysis

Role models: Malcolm Gladwell, Jordan Peterson (author of *12 Rules for Life*), Elon Musk, Theodore Geisel (Dr. Seuss)

Emotional Pillar

Feelings and relationships encompass the emotional pillar. Connection to others is a basic human need, but how much connection you enjoy can vary. You might want a large number of close friends who get together often. Or you might prefer quiet times with one special someone.

If you rate your emotional pillar as a 10, you see success in life based on the quality and number of strong relationships you have. You strike up friendships with colleagues, neighbors, and the guy behind the counter at your local coffee shop. You love networking and enjoy introducing people. You work at remembering names and details about people, so you can keep those connections going, even after long periods of no contact. You take care of others and enjoy making people feel special.

If you rank high on the emotional pillar, you probably:

- Value loyalty
- Give service without recognition
- Send Thank You notes
- Like, comment & share often on social media
- Feel grief over lost relationships as well as hold grudges

- Belong to networking clubs
- Let your feelings flow without holding back

Role Models: Mark Cuban (Shark Tank), Mick Jagger (Rolling Stones), Oprah Winfrey

Spiritual Pillar

Your connectedness with yourself, the earth and others makes up the spiritual pillar. This involves tapping into something greater than yourself and helping the world become a better place. This focus on the greater good is a hallmark of the spiritual pillar.

If your spiritual pillar is a 10 out of 10, you stay on the spiritual plane. You practice meditation and higher thinking and look at the bigger picture of the world and humanity.

If you rank high on the spiritual pillar, you probably:

- Focus on your inner being more than outside events
- Project love and acceptance to everyone
- Care about the wellbeing of the planet, animals and humans
- Bring a sense of stability to wherever you are
- Write inspiring books and articles

Role Models: Dali Lama, Mother Theresa, Eckhart Tolle, Depok Chopra

Financial Pillar

Money and career are the two primary elements of the financial pillar. Earning a living is part of it, but it also includes the ability to receive compensation and accept what you are due. As well as your propensity to invest and take financial risks.

If you know how to play the money game, your score on the financial pillar is a 10 out of 10. You love learning about how money works and what's working now. You belong to investment clubs, and you are constantly in tune with what your own money is doing and what the world economy is doing. You feel the same thrill when you score financially as a wide receiver going in for a touchdown.

If you rank high on the financial pillar, you probably:

- Pay yourself first
- Work to increase income
- Have multiple streams of income
- Watch current events as well as your own financial sheets
- Make skilled investments

Role Models: Kevin O'Leary (Shark Tank), Richard Branson, Grant Cardone

Rating and ranking each of these 5 areas provides valuable information for creating a happy, purpose-filled and productive life. If you rate a pillar as 10 out of 10, you are a superstar in that area. If you are great in that area, but not a superstar, you would rank yourself as an 8 or a 9. A rating of 1 means you don't care much about this pillar. I created a self-assessment that appears on the next page in order to help you create something tangible from all of this.

First, rate each pillar on a scale of 1-10 for how important each one is in your life like previously mentioned. Then think of how you can focus on that one to create a career and income stream. Conversely think about how you can strengthen your weakest pillar?

Rate each pillar below:	List pillars in order of importance:
_____ Physical	_____
_____ Mental	_____
_____ Emotional	_____
_____ Spiritual	_____
_____ Financial	_____

In column 2, rewrite the 5 pillars, ranking them from highest to lowest as they pertain to you personally.

If you have a tie at the top, first, double check and make sure your rankings are a legitimate tie. If you do have a legit tie, no sweat, this is actually great news. Combine those 2 pillars when thinking about how to implement them in your life. For example, if physical and mental are a tie, how can you blend them together, such as teaching new concepts about health, or showing people how to maximize their physical performance by expanding the mind. For a tie in emotional and financial, possibly blend these together with a career in fundraising for non-profits or teaching financial literacy to underprivileged people. Use your imagination and discover how to create full alignment between multiple areas of your life, you'll be astonished with what you can create.

Here are more examples of careers involving the 5 Pillars :

Physical —barbershop, nail salon, nutrition, diet coaching, biology, martial arts instructor, personal trainer

Mental —teacher, mentor, author, book editor, librarian, blogger

Emotional—social worker, caregiver, club leader, nanny, dating coach

Spiritual —meeting leader, spiritual adviser, speaker, humanitarian

Financial —investments, accountant, banker, real estate

These pillars are a broad guideline rather than a strict pathway or a rigid rulebook. They can help you clarify where you are and what your next steps might be. Keep in mind, as you progress through your life's journey, your rankings will change. It's helpful to revisit this self-assessment to see where you might be shifting as you learn more and experience more in your career or life's work.

With this information, you're ready to take the next step and monetize your top pillars. It's time for you to reach your potential and Live in Alignment!

SECTION 2

Make Money

Chapter 7

THE 4 CURRENCIES

Imagine for a moment that you're out in a field and you're tasked to build an entire house from scratch. In the grass lies a complete kit for the house—all the windows, doors, rafters, shingles, lumber, everything—including all the tools. Would you be able to build a strong stable house with your own two hands? Unless you've been a contractor, most of you will answer "no" to this question. However, the problem isn't a lack of tools, the problem is that nobody showed you how to use them. Money is a tool. Most people have the limiting belief that they need more "tools" to be successful financially. The truth is, if you have a bank account and a credit card, you already have all the tools you need to be financially fulfilled.

"It's not the lack of resources but the lack of resourcefulness that ultimately makes the difference."
~Tony Robbins

When asked the question: "What do you use as currency?" most will answer, "Money." While money is a common answer, money actually has a different definition than currency. Money is simply a byproduct of value exchange. Money is the most obvious medium of exchange but the word *currency* means <u>anything used</u> in a value exchange.

> "Money is simply a byproduct of value exchange."
> "Currency means anything used in a value exchange."

Successful people understand they can use much more than just money to create value. This is a key difference between the top 1% of the wealthy and the rest of the world. Sometimes our most powerful currency is not actually money. When I fully grasped this concept, I began to see a big jump in my own success.

A couple of years ago in a Real Estate seminar I attended, the trainer mentioned 4 types of currencies as a sidebar in his session. I Didn't think much of it at the time, but as soon as I started implementing these 4 Currencies myself, opportunities opened up for me like never before, and my entire view of money changed.

The 4 Currencies are:

Money
Time
Knowledge
Relationships

How a person uses the 4 Currencies will determine their level of success and display their current money mindset. We either operate from a place of high financial literacy or low financial literacy as determined by our money habits.

> "How a person uses the 4 Currencies depends on whether their financial literacy is low or high."

Low Financial Literacy

Recently, I was in a conversation with an Uber driver who showed how this works. I'll call him Harry. He was talkative and asked me what I did for a living. When he heard that I teach people about money, he asked for my advice. He told me he was in debt and constantly under money stress. Harry had started driving for Uber on nights and weekends, so he could pay his bills.

I asked him a few questions and discovered that Harry and his wife both had good jobs. Together, they were bringing in about $180,000 per year. They lived in a modest house with an average mortgage. Harry thought he had a money problem. What he actually had was a financial literacy problem.

> "Harry thought he had a money problem. What he actually had was a financial literacy problem."

Even though he was bringing in well over $100k as a household he still worked a 9-5 job and lived paycheck to paycheck. He dreaded getting up in the morning and lived for weekends and vacations. Harry thought he needed a windfall of money in order to get ahead. Because Harry believed the answer to his stress was more money, he used up all his time trying to get more money in a never-ending cycle.

Someone with low financial literacy will tend to use the 4 Currencies as follows:

1. **Money is the reason for their decisions and actions.** They work hard at a job they don't like in exchange for a paycheck. They live in a cycle of work for money.

2. **Time is a tool.** They use up their time to obtain money. When their time is all used up, the only way they can obtain more money is to try to get a pay raise.

3. **Knowledge is a burden.** They say, "I need to pass this test, so I can get my diploma or my certification for that job I want." Once they cross that milestone, they don't crack open a book again until the next class comes up, if it ever does.

4. **Relationships are competitive.** They don't want others to know what they have or what they are up to. If you were to ask them, "How much do you make?" or "How much are you worth?" they would likely say, "It's none of your business!" People with low financial literacy are suspicious of others who would like to work with them in a money venture.

The best part of living in this century is the availability of training. With the right information, someone with low financial literacy can switch their thinking and join the 1% where the game completely changes. My hope is that this book might serve as a catalyst to propel your money mindset in the right direction.

I was in the low financial literacy cycle, too, until one day I said, "Enough is enough. I can't take this rat race any longer," and I started educating myself to have high financial literacy like I mentioned in the previous chapters. Once I discovered the 4 Currencies, my relationship with money changed.

> "Once I discovered the 4 Currencies,
> my relationship with money changed."

High Financial Literacy

Here's how the 1% implements the 4 Currencies:

1. **Money is a tool.**

   They use money to buy as much time as possible.

   As an example, at the age of 22, I was a leasing agent for a property group in downtown Philadelphia. From my perspective, I had a lot of money coming in via my paycheck. What I didn't have was a lot of time. I used my money currency to pay people who had time. They put out fliers for me while I was at work and helped me get more business. My money currency was high and my time currency was low so I found someone who had the opposite and was able to create a win/win scenario.

   > "Use money to pay people who have time."

2. **Time is the reason behind their actions and decisions.**

   Time is the most valuable currency, the more a person maximizes time, the more successful they will be. They spend the other 3 currencies to get more time.

During my mastermind , I often hear members say they want to start a business, but they don't have time because of working a job. I tell them, "That's great. You have money currency to pay someone to free up your time." This could be hiring a lawncare service, paying someone to make follow-up phone calls, or having a social media company take care of your online presence. Use money to relieve you of the tedious tasks that drain your time. Then you can focus your time on your business.

"Utilize money to get more time."

3. **Knowledge is a constant journey.**

To the 1% every day is an exploration to find more knowledge.

In his article, "Bill Gates, Warren Buffett, And Oprah All Use The 5-Hour Rule," author Michael Simmons says to consider the extreme reading habits of billionaire entrepreneurs:

- Warren Buffett spends five to six hours per day reading five newspapers and 500 pages of corporate reports.
- Bill Gates reads 50 books per year.
- Mark Zuckerberg reads at least one book every two weeks.
- Elon Musk grew up reading two books a day, according to his brother.
- Mark Cuban reads more than 3 hours every day.
- Arthur Blank, co-founder of Home Depot, reads two hours a day.

- Billionaire entrepreneur David Rubenstein reads six books a week.
- Dan Gilbert, self-made billionaire and owner of the Cleveland Cavaliers, reads one to two hours a day. [2]

Successful people know that continuous learning gives them knowledge they can use as currency. Think of how much an expert in a field can earn in one hour compared to an employee's pay for one hour. The difference is exponential—with zeros behind the expert's number.

I experience this with my mastermind. With even a $500 trial price and only 5 attendees, I can earn $2500 for an hour of teaching compared to $25 for that same hour as an employee and still deliver $25,000 worth of value to the members, win/win.

"Gain knowledge like it's money in the bank."

4. **Relationships are collaborative.**

Rich people hang out with others who talk about money and invite conversations about ways to pool resources for the benefit of everyone involved. Their ability to leverage relationships relies on trust, so they understand the importance of maintaining trust with each other.

When I want more relationships, I trade my money for access to a group of likeminded people. If I didn't have

---

2   Michael Simmons, "Bill Gates, Warren Buffett, and Oprah all use the 5-hour rule," Medium.com, July 26, 2016.

money, I might trade my time instead and hang out in places where those people frequent—such as networking events or webinars—and let relationships develop.

"Businesses are built on relationship currency."

For example, when members ask for real estate advice in my mastermind I often tell them that Real Estate is not a house business, it's a people business. Think about it, you need contractors, investors, a title company, a Real Estate broker, appraisers, inspectors, the list goes on and on. When you build relationships with key players opportunities come to you first and much more frequently. Relationships are golden. The same is true in any business.

If I need more of one currency, I use the other 3 currencies to support the weakest link. If I needed more knowledge, I'd pay someone with that knowledge to fill in the gaps for me—such as a lawyer or a contractor. If I needed more money, I could use my knowledge to turn time and relationships into funding—such as spending a morning calling colleagues and finding investors.

When I discovered the power of the 4 currencies my money mindset expanded and I stopped seeing my needs as a roadblock and started seeing them as a puzzle I could solve. That's when opportunities started showing up in abundance.

"I stopped seeing my needs as a roadblock
and started seeing them as a puzzle I could solve."

Tasks, Time And Money

Let's look at some ways you can use the 4 currencies to trade a lower-value task for a higher-value task. For example, let's say, you are a stock trader, making big deals all day long. You are trading your time for money. Paying a driver to take you to meetings could allow you to continue making deals while in route. Hypothetically, let's say you spend $50 or $100 for a lower-value task (driving), and you can make $2500 or $25,000 from a higher-value task (making deals). Congratulations you just increased your income by recognizing and understanding the value of the 4 currencies.

Many times we forget to value our time and only value our money. Handing the work off to another person or system can actually make us more money when done correctly.

These types of value-based decisions create the lifestyle of the rich. Think of the time saved by a private jet rather than dealing with airport security and long waits at the baggage claim. Sure, the luxury is nice, but more important than soft lounge chairs and brass-rimmed cupholders is time. Time is the currency the 1% values most.

When faced with a task, I immediately think about it from two angles:

First, how can I delegate or offset this task and still produce the intended result? Can I hire someone else? Can I put a system in place to automate or speed things up?

Second, what's my ROI on this task? In the example of hiring a driver, if I can spend $50 to cover a mundane task, so I can make $2500, I'll do that all day long.

The same goes for hiring outside vendors. For example, a bookkeeper can take the spreadsheets off my plate, so I have more time to gather knowledge, to develop relationships and close deals. A marketing company could give me their knowledge about branding to bring my company to the notice of bigger players and improve the quality of my business relationships. The 4 Currencies ebb and flow together in a fascinating matrix of value.

"The 4 Currencies ebb and flow together in a fascinating matrix of value."

Accumulation vs. Cash Flow

People with low financial literacy often compete to accumulate more stuff—a big bank account, a mansion, a Porsche and extended European vacations three times a year. They believe more stuff means they're more successful than their neighbor. Those with a high financial literacy play a different game entirely. For them, it's not about accumulation, it's about cashflow.

Accumulation is not the way to wealth, Cashflow is. Think of accumulation as a gallon jug of water whereas cashflow is more like a running faucet. Sure, the gallon might appear larger at first sight but the jug will eventually run out of water, it's capacity is limited. The faucet—even if it's only dripping—wins all day long, it's capacity is limitless.

It's time to break out of the accumulation game and get into the cashflow game. If you want to create financial fulfillment begin thinking in terms of cashflow and stop worrying about accumulation.

"Accumulation is not the way to wealth, Cash flow is."

Taking this to a more practical application, when we play the low financial literacy game, we become slaves to the system made up by the government, banks and corporations. These institutions tell us that we should be employees and think in terms of 9-5 jobs, W-2's and paychecks. People in this system work under their Social Security number and hope they will accumulate enough for retirement. They buy liabilities (houses, cars and other toys) that take money out of their pocket.

Those of us who have high financial literacy see the world differently. We occupy a world made up of investors, owners and controllers. Using 1099s, EIN numbers, write offs, and passive cash flow we generate income around the clock. We invest in assets, work on things we are passionate about, and are constantly learning and looking for valuable relationships.

In order to fully optimize the 4 Currencies we first need to understand opportunity. Most people think there is only one step to opportunity: "Take advantage of it when it comes by." In reality there are 3 steps to opportunity, when you fully grasp them you'll be able to take full advantage of them. The 3 steps to opportunity are:

1. **Change your environment.** When you know what you are looking for, you can place yourself in environments where opportunities are likely to be more abundant. For example, if your passion is Real Estate, attending meetings with other Real Estate investors will put you in an environment where opportunities abound.

2. **Become aware of opportunities when they show up.** Opportunities are often more elusive than we think.

Say, you want $100. Instead of looking at the ground, hoping to find a bill someone dropped, you might meet someone who has a currency that you can leverage to make $100. You might have to negotiate and work it out, but using your awareness, your knowledge and ingenuity, you can reach your goal.

3. **Take advantage of the opportunities.** Knowing the 4 Currencies means you'll have clarity on the value you offer and the value you receive and how to leverage it. You can take advantage of opportunities with confidence.

When looking for opportunities for partnerships or Joint ventures, taking the 4 Currencies into account will allow you to understand if there is value for you or not. It also helps you decide how to best structure the venture. One person might have key relationships to find opportunities, while another has experience and brings knowledge to the table. Maybe a third person writes grants, so they have access to funding. A strong presence in all 4 Currencies will likely make the venture more successful.

> "A strong presence in all 4 Currencies
> will make the venture more successful."

When you expand your thinking to include all 4 Currencies, the road to wealth becomes wider and more accessible. Instead of staying stuck looking at money, check into other areas where you have something to offer, invite collaborations from those who have a currency you need and stay alert for opportunities.

Chapter 8

THE NEW GOLD

The Number One excuse I hear people make when they start their wealth journey is: "I don't have enough money." We've already talked about other currencies aside from money, but taking it one step further, let's look at money from a different perspective. The way most people think about increasing their financial health is by saving more money each month and building their cash savings. You might not realize this, but access to cash is just as important as having cash itself .

It is highly unlikely that you will ever be able to save your way to wealth, so let's look at a different strategy. Here's why credit is much better than cash in my opinion.

> "It is highly unlikely that you will ever
> be able to save your way to wealth."

Credit is Faster

If you saved $100 per month for 12 months, you'd have $1200 in one year. If you work at increasing your credit limit, you can 20x your credit limit in that same 12 months, like I did. If you begin the year with just $5000 in available credit, you could have access to $100,000 by the end of the year.

Your credit limit will always grow faster than your savings account ever could. It will take you much further in less time, so be strategic and build your access to cash.

> "Your credit limit will always grow faster
> than your savings account ever could."

When it comes to credit, you might be immediately inclined to think in terms of Credit Score. To be frank, you have been fed a lie when it comes to credit scores and their importance. If you're like most people, you treat your credit score as a trophy to sit on a dresser as a status symbol. This belief is not only false, but it's causing you to leave money on the table.

I'm here to tell you that three hundred dollars will always buy more than an 850 credit score. At first this might seem confusing but let me paint a picture. Imagine you and I are shopping at a grocery store. I'll bring $300 dollars in cash, and you bring your perfect 850 credit score. Let's see who can buy more groceries.

A credit score does not equal purchasing power. In fact, if you told me you have an 850 credit score, I would tell you, "You have a wasted score!"

> "A credit score does not equal purchasing power."

Banks see little difference between an 850 and 750 credit score. If you have a 750 score you will qualify for the same loan as if you had an 850. Banks and lending institutions place borrowers into tiers, and the top lending tier ranges between high 700s to 850. You don't need a perfect 850 score to get where you want to go. Working for a perfect 850 is actually leaving money on the table.

Now that we have debunked the Credit Score Myth, let's find some money!

Cash Flow Not Accumulation

If your plan is to build up your savings until you have enough to invest, you are practicing accumulation. That's a Low Financial Literacy approach that will get you nowhere like we mentioned in the last chapter. This also applies to net worth. When people talk about net worth, they are referring to value that's locked into property and assets they don't have immediate access to. To me, net worth is like having a safe full of cash without the combination to unlock it. You'll need a lot of time and effort to get that cash into your hands so you can use it.

> "If your plan is to build up your savings until you have enough to invest, you are practicing accumulation."

Instead of accumulation, it's time to turn on the money faucet—even if it's only a drip—and let the cash flow.

To me, savings accounts are like diets. Most people stay with it for two weeks, and then they fall off—the car breaks down, an emergency flight across the country to go to a sick loved one, or maybe you can't resist a sad-eyed puppy on the rescue website. When stuff happens, you'll likely fall off the wagon.

Instead of relying on deprivation and raw willpower, why not use strategic methods that focus on abundance and living a life you love?

Fast Track to Cash

The way to get access to more and more credit is to apply, apply, apply for more cards and credit increases on the cards you have. However, first learn the ins and outs of handling credit effectively. Credit is powerful. If this is your first jump, get a mentor and jump out of the plane with him or her at your back.

Before going further into funding strategies, it's important for you to understand the different aspects of credit, starting with your credit score. I know, earlier I told you not to worry about credit score. However, you need to understand some basics first because this topic has a lot of misunderstandings. I'm giving you the real scoop here. Even if you think you know all about credit, keep reading because you won't find what I'm about to teach you in an economics book.

"Even if you think you know all about credit, keep reading."

Credit involves three things:

1. Credit scores
2. Credit bureaus
3. Credit reports

Credit Scores

First things first, NOBODY has a credit Score. Yes, you heard me correctly. Credit scores are not attached to individuals. They are attached to credit reports, which we will get to soon. Every credit report has multiple scores at any given time.

Credit reports have a multitude of scoring models. The two most common are FICO and Vantage Score. When it comes to applying for credit, the model you'll need to focus on is FICO.

"The two most common credit models are FICO and Vantage Score."

FICO has various scoring versions, numbered as FICO 8, 9, 10, etc. Each version is based on lender criteria. Each version puts emphasis on specific things. In the credit industry, they say each version is weighted differently.

"FICO has various scoring versions, numbered as FICO 8, 9, 10, etc."

For example, have you ever had a scenario where you went to the bank, checked your credit score, and the bank official tells you the score is 710? Immediately, you leave the bank and head to the car lot to finance a new car. The car lot pulls a 675 score. You shake your head because you hadn't so much as stopped for a burger on the way over. What happened?

The reason: the bank probably gave out your Unweighted score and the car lot pulled an Auto-Weighted score and who knows which version each pulled. Different lending activities have different weights, including Auto Loans, Home Loans and Bank Cards.

"Different lending activities have different weights."

I'll explain scoring in more detail later, but for now let's talk about credit bureaus.

Credit Bureaus

Credit bureaus have one job: collecting data. Although hundreds of credit bureaus are out there, the three main ones are Experian, Equifax, and Transunion. These bureaus generate up-to-date credit reports on borrowers. They know your credit limits and the balances currently on those accounts. They know whether you pay on time or late, and whether you have defaulted at some point and have accounts in collections. They also know when a lender checks your score to see if you qualify for more credit.

These reports help determine your likelihood of approval. Each report has a FICO score that comes from its corresponding model, version and weight.

Credit Reports

Five factors make up your credit report:

1. Payment History: are your payments on time or late?
2. Utilization Ratio: what percentage of your available credit are you actually accessing?
3. Age of Credit: how old is your oldest account and newest account?
4. Mix of Credit: do you have a cross section of car, home, lines of credit, cards and personal loans?

5. Inquiries: how often have you recently tried to get new credit?

Each of these five factors receive a value based on your performance as a borrower. Together they create your FICO score. FICO Scores range from 300-850. To simplify the math, start at zero instead of 300 and say the range is 0-550. This way you can figure out how much weight each area of your report carries.

Payment history is 35% of your report: 550 x 35% = 192.5. This means you can lose a maximum of 192.5 points if you have a terrible payment history. Making those minimum payments on time is the most important aspect of your score. If you're 30 Days late, you lose a few points, 60 Days later, you lose more and 90 Days late you can lose a lot of points.

Utilization Ratio is 30% of your report: 550 x 30% = 165. You can lose a maximum of 165 points if you have maxed out cards. To keep your score high, use less than 30% of your available credit. This is a balancing act, and I'll get to that later in the chapter.

Age of Credit is 15% of your report: 550 x 15% = 82.5 points. To find your Age of Credit, add the length of your oldest credit and your newest credit, then divide by the number of credit accounts.

Mix of Credit is 10% of your report: 550 x 10% = 55 points. Instead of focusing on credit cards, apply for lines of credit and other types of loans to keep this value high.

Hard inquiries are 10% of your credit report: 550 x 10% = 55 points. When you submit an application, the lender's system checks your credit score. This is called a hard inquiry. The credit bureau makes a note in your report whenever this happens, so lenders can see if you are actively looking for more credit.

When applying for credit cards, don't worry about hard inquiries on your report. If you get approved, your credit limit will go up, and your utilization ratio will go down. In other words, you could lose points for the hard inquiry, but you can also gain points if your credit limit goes up.

> "When applying for credit cards
> don't worry about hard inquiries on your report."

Here are some numbers to show what I mean:

Let's say you have $2000 in available credit, and you have a $1000 balance (money owed) on your credit cards. Your utilization percentage is 50%.

Let's say you apply for a new card and get a credit increase of $8,000. Now your total limit is $10,000 and you owe $1000, so your utilization ratio just dropped to 10% without paying one penny on your balance!

You might lose 10 points because of the hard inquiry, but you could also gain 25 points when you're accepted. In a situation where you're in a good place for an increase, applying for more credit could be worth the decrease for the hard inquiry. Those hard-inquiry hits also expire fairly quickly.

> "You might lose 10 points because of the hard inquiry,
> but you could also gain 25 points when you're accepted."

How Credit Applications Work

Let's imagine a man named John Smith decides he wants to increase his credit limit by opening a new credit card. He's taking an investment class and now's the time for him to take action.

He walks into his bank and asks for a credit card. The bank official has John fill out an application. Once he completes his application, the bank official submits the application to the credit bureau, let's say Equifax, for example.

The system produces John's most up-to-date credit report and Equifax, using the FICO scoring model, assigns the correct version and weight that matches John's request for a credit card. It scores him at 738.

Equifax then sends John's credit report to the bank. The bank official enters John's application and credit report into their computer system to begin the automatic underwriting process. The bank's underwriting algorithms check John's information and either (1) fully approve his request, (2) deny his request or (3) approve for a lesser amount.

Sometimes, the computer will kick out the application because the data isn't clear enough for an automatic decision. In this case, a bank employee in the underwriting office will take a look and make a decision. At the end of the application process, John receives a notice that he is approved or he'll get a letter in the mail saying he was declined and why.

When your goal is raising your credit limit, take steps to qualify through the automatic system by making minimum payments on time and keeping your usage low. This will increase your likelihood of instant access to more funding.

"When your goal is raising your credit limit,
take steps to qualify through the automatic system."

As you work your plan, you will be able to act on opportunities and see a return that covers the cost and goes far beyond while minimizing the risk. In the following chapter I'm taking a deeper dive into credit and how I advise using it. Keep Going ☺

Chapter 9

REDEFINE RISK

When it comes debt and credit, I see two camps:

First, the live-debt-free person who avoids debt by fully paying off any cards they might have. They want to reduce the number of open credit accounts in their portfolio as soon as possible. They see credit and debt as a weight and far too risky unless they are making a house payment or keeping a card open for emergencies.

Second, the use-debt-as-a-tool person who uses debt to create cash flow. They have a strategy when it comes to using their lines of credit or credit cards, so they don't see debt as risky but as their means of doing business. This is a High Financial Literacy strategy that takes some learning.

Before increasing your credit limit, sit down and think about your goal for the money you are about to access. In six months from now, how will your ROI pay the bill on a six-figure balance? Make plans for covering this cost to prevent problems in the future. You've heard the stories of people who win the lottery and are broke the next year. Don't let this be you.

"Think about your goal for this money."

My recommendation is to only use credit for assets and emergencies. If you have a $100,000 accident, having open credit to cover it will relieve a lot of stress. In addition to that, I encourage my clients to purchase training and mentor programs that will increase their income far more than the cost. Make investments with a positive return. I don't advise buying liabilities with credit.

"I don't advise buying liabilities with credit."

As a hypothetical example, if I have $100,000 in available credit, I can purchase a rental property for $50,000. Let's say my credit card bill for the $50,000 is $650 per month, but I rent the property out for $1500. I am no longer making the $650 payment each month because my tenant is paying it. I'm also collecting $850 minus expenses on top of that.

Take it one step further. If you buy that $50,000 house to rehab it, you might put $30,000 on your Home Depot card for the rehab. Once the rehab is finished, you can refinance the house and get tax-free cash out. From that, you can pay off your credit cards and still rent the house for $1500 per month for cash flow or sell it and get more cash out right away.

Add some zeroes to these deals and maybe you have $1,000,000 in available credit and purchase an investment property for $500,000. The same principles apply. Where you are in your experience and your perspective determines the level you play at. The strategies are largely the same.

This is why I love credit cards so much and why I focus on credit limits instead of scores. When you understand how to create this kind of ROI and have a goal in mind from the start, credit becomes as valuable as gold! This is how credit works for you.

You might see all those zeroes and get scared. At the beginning, you need a mentor to help you navigate. It's also where you blast through your Low Financial Literacy limiting beliefs and expand into the High Financial Literacy wealth mindset. Those zeroes are only risky when you aren't clear on your strategy and your goal. Remember, credit is simply money with terms.

In my experience, there's no such thing as a risky investment, only risky investors. Let me show you what I mean.

"There's no such thing as a risky investment, only risky investors."

Let's say you have two humans and one gun. The first person is a 13-year-old kid who is going to the shooting range with his father for the first time. The gun feels heavy and clumsy in his hands. He isn't sure where to touch the various parts of the gun and where to avoid touching it. He sort of aims but isn't exactly sure what he's looking at. When he shoots, the recoil brings the gun back. It knocks him in the face, leaving his cheekbone bruised and bleeding.

The second person is the kid's father who is a Marine veteran of two Gulf wars. He picks up the same weapon with ease. He knows every knob and switch on the gun because he can take it apart and put it together blindfolded in under thirty seconds. He sights and aims almost instantaneously, shoots a bull's eye and then another and another.

When they leave the shooting range, the kid thinks, "Wow. Guns are risky." His dad has the gun safely tucked away and doesn't give it much thought. To him, it's all in a day's work.

Is the gun itself risky or does the risk come from the user? The level of risk comes from the amount of education the person has. Someone with no training can bumble around and create a lot of chaos in short order. Someone trained knows how to minimize risk until it's not a major issue.

The same is true of debt. Someone who is untrained sees only danger, while a trained investor who knows how to use debt effectively sees it as a useful tool for the right place and the right time. That's not to say debt has no danger. Yes, danger does exist, but people get overwhelmed with debt by mishandling credit. Used correctly, credit and debt can be the pipeline for positive cash flow in a short amount of time.

> "Used correctly, credit and debt can be the pipeline for positive cash flow in a short amount of time."

While people with Low Financial Literacy look at debt as the problem, those with High Financial Literacy know that negative cash flow is the real problem. Using credit and debt strategically, they become the ticket to financial independence faster, better and easier than other methods, especially for someone starting out.

I've been using these techniques for years now, and they have been pivotal in expediting my progress toward financial independence. However, I've also seen people stumble because they didn't have the right information, or they were trying to go it alone without someone to guide them. Here are a few things to watch out for.

What NOT to Do

1. **Don't start without a solid reason.**

   Why are you building up your credit limit? What is your strategy? Do you have a plan with a goal in mind?

2. **Don't apply for store cards and mall cards**.

   Store cards only give you product, not cash. They buy liabilities and accumulate debt. Major credit cards like VISA and MasterCard will increase your access to funding that brings a return on investment.

   If you are a Real Estate investor, two exceptions would be Lowes˚ and Home Depot˚. These store cards cover renovations or improvements for Real Estate investments. Investment lenders like to see that you have these two cards in your portfolio, so these accounts will open doors for you to get even more funding. Some investors will turn you down if you don't have them.

   The only other exception I will make is an Amazon credit card simply because Amazon sells practically everything, including food, during extreme emergencies.

3. **Don't pay high interest rates.**

   Keep transferring debt to new cards with 0% interest, usually 12-15 months. I call this *debt arbitrage* because I keep an eye on my monthly payments to make sure I'm paying the card companies less than my monthly ROI.

If I pay out $300 on the cards and bring $600 into my bank account every month, I can keep doing that forever. Note: If credit card companies see you moving money around with these transfers, they could start turning you down for increases. However, if you are using your credit strategically to bring in more cash, more increases become less important. You can ride the wave, work your plan until you get a larger payout, then pay down your balances and start again.

Maintaining Your Financial Health

When working with new mastermind members, I see a frequent pitfall, especially after a few weeks. Almost every time, one or more members will ask me whether they still need their accountant now that they know how money works. They wonder if they should start doing their own books and filing their own taxes.

I ask if it makes sense to fire their doctor and perform surgery on themselves.

When they say, "Of course not!" I ask, "Why would you continue to hire a professional for your physical health but fire the professional when it comes to your financial health?"

> "Why hire a professional for your physical health but fire the professional for your financial health?"

Knowledge is important, and financial advice is equally as important as medical advice. I see it all the time where someone will take the advice of the first financial planner they come across as though one adviser is as good as another.

If you want to do something successfully, work with someone who has done that activity successfully and model them. Finding the best minds to help you with your strategy and implementation is crucial to keeping risk low.

> *"Successful people seek counsel, failures listen to opinion."*
> ~Greg Reid

I ran headlong into this idea of risk in 2018.

From the time I was eighteen years old, I knew I wanted to be an entrepreneur. By the time I was twenty-three I had realized my dream of starting a Real Estate investing business, and I acquired investment properties.

About a year in, I ran into a string of Murphy's Law events over a three-month period. I'd put out one fire and another more-expensive blaze would spring up. At the time, I didn't have a savings account or a lot of cash reserves or a significant amount of credit.

The day came when I realized I was completely broke. Actually, I was negative $2,000 at the bank and counting. At that point I went to my usual go to—lenders and credit. I immediately learned that when you need money, no one will give you a loan.

I was rock-star material a few months before, but now I was the ugliest person in the night club, and no one would dance with me.

When you don't need money, lenders will beg you to borrow from them. Credit card applications come in the mail, tele-marketers and emails will let you know you qualify for more and more credit. That changed the moment I ran out of money.

"When you don't need money,
lenders will beg you to borrow from them."

My house of cards was about to fall. I went into crisis management mode. I begged, pleaded and looked for personal loans to pull me out of the quicksand. After ten or eleven calls to money lenders, I told the last guy, "I have a house for you to refinance."

He started with the usual questions: "How much cash reserve do you have? What's your credit score? Do you have any assets?"

I stopped him and said, "I'm not going to fit any of your credentials. If you'll work with me, you'll get paid on the back end when I have other deals coming through. All I need is a push to get past this situation. Everyone else already told me no."

Somehow, I caught a break, and he agreed. At the same time, I got a job with an income of $250 per week (which was much better than the negative $2,000 in my bank account). I started to pull away from the disaster zone.

After I climbed out of that hole, I focused on creating a net for myself. If another series of Murphy's Law events were to hit me, I would weather the storm using my own credit. No more begging unwilling partners to dance with me.

If another series of Murphy's Law events were to hit me,
I would weather the storm using my own credit."

Before my string of bad luck, I had $4,000 in available credit. I was one emergency away from being 100% utilized. Because of that experience, I learned some money hacks that took me from $4,000 to $85,000 in available credit in 12 months. Most people would take 12 years to have that increase if they try to save. As a result, I had an emergency fund that could withstand most anything that came along, and from there I have continued to grow my cash flow.

Now's a good time to take a breath and check in on your own relationship with risk. Do you have a backup plan for those Murphy's Law moments? Are you growing your safety net so you can weather the down times? On the following pages are some money hacks that will help you get started.

Chapter 10

MONEY HACKS

A s with every industry, money has its own set of hacks. The *status quo* is usually not the best way to go. Common sense is not always common practice. Here are a few hacks that have simplified my life, helped me scale my business with a bigger safety net and shown me the way to success.

1. **If you see a coin on the ground...PICK IT UP!**

My friend and mentor, Larry Steinhouse has a solid rule: any money lying on the ground within his eyesight goes straight into his pocket. If you happen to be with Larry and you step over a penny, he'll yell, "What the heck are you doing, ? If you'll step over pennies, you'll step over dollars. You'll leave money on the table, too."

Larry tells the story about the time he and his wife, Linda, were on the train to New York City. They were looking forward to an evening of fine dining at The Capitol Grille and dressed for the part. Larry is known for his style, and tonight was a 5-star night all the way around.

During the trip, Larry noticed two pennies lying in the aisle, one to the right and one to the left. He nudged Linda, and they made a deal. As they were leaving the train, he would get the one on the left, and she would get the one on the right.

That started a chain of events neither of them expected.

The moment Larry bent over to pick up the penny, his pants split from top to bottom. His ankles felt the cold. He grabbed the penny and stood up, thanking the style gods that he had worn a long jacket.

When they came out of Central Station, they headed straight to Macy's where he found a pair of pants, tore off the tags and put them on. He told the story to the attendant and handed him the penny to pay for the pants.

Like Larry says, stepping over money is a mindset. The next time you see money on the ground, pick it up, and reinforce your resolve to never leave money on the table.

"Stepping over money is a mindset."

2. Carry blank checks in your wallet.

Always be prepared to make a deal anywhere, day or night. You might be winding down at happy hour when the very guy you've been calling for days suddenly shows up. Not only can you talk to him, but you can also seal the deal because you have a check with you.

This is also a good negotiation tool. When someone is waffling on agreeing to a sale price, pulling out a blank check adds a lot of weight to your offer. It's also helpful to have a check when you're in town and you think of something you've been meaning to take care of. If you're prepared, you can drive into the parking lot, write a check and head on your way.

I've used this one more times than I can count. As a bonus tip I would also recommend downloading every payment app available. The options are practically limitless today with Venmo, Cashapp, Zelle, Apple Pay, Google Pay, etc. etc. it's important to make sure you have them all. Numerous times I've encountered the situation where I have a different app than my potential customer, not anymore! Additionally, I would also recommend getting the debit cards associated with each, the ease and convenience of accessing your cash through them is essential.

"Always be prepared to make a deal anywhere, day or night."

3. **Ask and ask again.**

In my classes, so many people say to me, "I went to the bank, and they turned me down." My response: "Well, find another bank!"

In certain districts, you'll find half-a-dozen or more banks within a small radius. Keep walking and asking. If one says no, ask why. Take that information, up your game at the next place, and keep on asking. You're not a failure unless you give up. Banks can only turn you down for so many reasons, be sure to make adjustments before heading to the next bank, take the information they gave you and apply the proper steps to increase your chances at the next bank.

"You're not a failure unless you give up."

4. **Never sell yourself before you're sold.**

During my mastermind, members will bring their deals to the table looking for feedback. Myself, or another member might ask, "Did you talk with them about "X" Strategy?" and the member seeking counsel will say, "Well, they're in a situation, so they wouldn't want to do that."

The reply is always: "How do you know without asking?"

Always ask. You don't know the answer until you ask.

"Always ask. You don't know the answer until you ask."

The same holds true for any negotiation. You might see someone who is your ideal client while you're walking your dog in the park, but you don't approach them because you've got mud on your shoes. The mud gives you an excuse for the deeper reason that you're timid and expecting rejection. Guys do this kind of thing all the time when they see a pretty girl and tell themselves they can't talk to her because they need a haircut… or they have a coffee stain on their shirt…or they left their lucky coin at home. Any excuse will do.

Who knows, that coffee stain could be a funny conversation starter like, "I wasn't going to come over because I have this coffee stain on my shirt, but I figured, *What the hay, it was good coffee.*" If she laughs, you have a reason to keep talking.

Don't hold back. Ask all the questions, and don't assume anything. A no is just a signal to try again. Also, don't be afraid to ask someone who has told you no, "What would it take to get you to say yes?" Sometimes they will provide key insight to either turn this conversation around or better prepare you for the next conversation. Don't be so afraid of rejection or so reliant on the perfect circumstances that you pass up on opportunities and don't ask. This is a key point. If you can get out of your own way, you'll find a lot more money.

"If you can get out of your own way, you'll find a lot more money."

Credit Hacks

Credit can be tricky. Knowing the finer points of how credit works can help you navigate the system, so it works for you.

1. **Moving money from credit to cash**

   If you've ever bought property, one of the first things you find out is that banks won't take credit cards as down payment. So, how can you turn $100,000 worth of credit into cash to buy Real Estate? Here's the hack:

   1. Open two PayPal accounts, one for business and one for personal.
   2. Have your business account invoice your personal account for the amount you need.
   3. From your personal account, use your credit card to pay that business invoice.
   4. Your funds just went from credit to cash.

   This is how I use my credit cards to buy Real Estate and other high-ticket purchases. Check out my Credit playlist on YouTube where you'll find the video: "Buying Real Estate with Credit Cards."

https://www.youtube.com/c/fredposimo

2. **Loans and lines**

Two lending instruments banks have for their customers are loans and lines of credit.

A loan is for a specific purpose, such as a house or a car. The money you receive is designated, and you must use it for that purpose. A loan is one-directional. When you pay it down, you're done. If you want more money, you have to reapply and go through all the steps again.

A line of credit is two-directional and often open to your discretion. It's replenishable. When you pay off the balances, the full amount automatically becomes available to you again. Credit cards are lines of credit attached to plastic cards. If you have $500 in cash, you can spend it once. If you have $500 in a line of credit, you have $500 forever, as long as you keep paying it back.

3. **Different types of interest**

In the U.S., most people believe a myth that the number on the interest rate determines how much you have to pay back. With a 5% mortgage and a 25% credit card, you might assume the credit card is more expensive to pay off because it has a bigger percentage. Comparing percentages is not apples-to-apples because the types of interest vary in how they are figured.

A card has an Annual Percentage Rate (APR) with an average daily balance. A mortgage is an amortized rate which is calculated much differently. You might end up paying a lot more for a 5% mortgage than a credit card at 25%. To understand the agreement you are making, look at the dollar amounts in actual numbers instead of simply choosing the lowest interest rate.

4. **Understand arbitrage**

According to *Websters Pocket Dictionary*, 4th Edition, arbitrage means the simultaneous purchase and sale in two markets. Some people might call this concept flipping. When you buy something at a yard sale and sell it on eBay for profit, that's retail arbitrage. I like to think of arbitrage as spending 3 in order to make 6.

An easy example is money lenders who borrow money at 6%, then lend that money at 8%. The additional 2% is lending arbitrage.

Let's say I borrow $50,000 at 8% interest to make a Real Estate investment. Three months later, I flip that house and sell it for $150,000. After everything is settled, I clear $25,000 in Real Estate arbitrage.

The lender in this instance borrowed that money at 6% interest. When I pay off the loan at 8%, he makes 2% on that transaction in arbitrage. Those are simplified numbers as a teaching point. The actual numbers rely on interest tables and other factors, of course.

With experience, money and credit hacks become second nature. You might discover some of them on your own, or you could learn them at lunch with a colleague or in an investment club. Pay attention, so you can note them down and practice them, the same as a surgeon refining a new technique. Money is your craft. Fine tune it and stay sharp.

For more money hacks, visit my website at www.MakeMoneyandHaveFun.com.

Chapter 11

THE MISSING ELEMENT

Now that you've made it this far through the book, you know the difference between assets and liabilities. You understand the 4 Currencies and the difference between spending time-for-money and spending money-for-time as well as the 5 Pillars of Life.

You know more about how the wealthy 1% think and what High Financial Literacy means. Notice, High Financial Literacy is not connected to how much net worth or income someone has. Many sports superstars and movie celebrities make millions but have Low Financial Literacy and squander their income on liabilities.

Remember the example: a bankrupt truck driver who takes a money course might have zero dollars at that moment, but with his new High Financial Literacy he will soon create cashflow. His financial potential is lightyears ahead of those in the Low Financial Literacy column, regardless of his cash on hand.

Here's an easy-read version of what we've learned so far about the basic differences between Low Financial Literacy and High Financial Literacy:

Low Financial Literacy	High Financial Literacy
• 9-5 jobs, W-2, paychecks	• 1099s, write-offs, passive income
• Slave to the system	• Work from passion and purpose
• Money buys liabilities	• Money buys time and assets
• Knowledge is a burden	• Knowledge is a journey
• Relationships are competitive	• Relationships are collaborative
• Tasks are inevitable drudgery	• Tasks are a time trade off
• Focus on accumulation	• Focus on cashflow
• Saving for retirement	• Retirement = cashflow
• Endure the environment	• Create a supportive environment
• Opportunities pass me by	• Opportunities are all around me
• Credit is a trap	• Credit is a tool
• Money topics overwhelm me	• Money is exciting to study
• Spend for gratification	• Strategically spend for ROI
• Investments are risky	• Investments are lucrative

While I definitely agree that studying and understanding money is vital to success, yet it's worth noting that in my discussions with millionaires, I've found that many people who are financially comfortable still have a sense of dissatisfaction. Have you ever come across someone making 6- or 7-figures who still feels miserable? They have an idea lurking in the back of their mind: *Is this all there is?* I call the answer to this question—The Missing Element.

Creating an abundant life is a three-step process.

Step One: Learning how to make money
Step Two: Identifying your passion that's also fun for you
Step Three: Having fun while you're making money

Most people stay on the first step, not realizing that so much more is waiting for them.

All this comes down to your mindset at the very core of your human experience, based on your philosophies, your belief systems and some things that—up until now—you've been completely certain about money. To up level the fun-factor in your relationship with money, you will need to change how you see the world and how you navigate through it.

In my own journey to getting acquainted with money, to understanding its nuances and what money really is, I've come to realize that money is actually an idea. To someone fresh from the Amazon jungle who has never been to civilization, those scraps of colored paper are pretty worthless until they realize the benefit of money via value exchange.

"Money is actually an idea."

Give a typical five-year-old a dollar, and all he sees is a toy or candy. That's what the value potential is to him. Adults, on the other hand, have a whole spectrum of value potentials when it comes to money. For some it means a new car every two years. For others, it means investments with cashflow returns. Having more money might even mean having more time, or making the family happy with gifts and experiences.

Then, there's another type of person to whom money means nothing more than a lump under the mattress or a bigger number at the bottom of an account balance. They don't buy toys or go on vacations. They see all investments as being too risky. For these people, money doesn't do them much good, other than a sense of satisfaction when they turn over at night and feel that lump hit them in the side. When that person leaves this life, someone else will collect that cash and apply their own pie slices as they wish. The real value of money is in its exchange.

"The real value of money is in its exchange."

While moving into the High Financial Literacy column is important, I also want to be happy and have fun, don't you? What good is a lumpy mattress if you don't enjoy life?

What does fun look like to you? What makes you happy, and what makes you miserable? For one person, showing houses to potential buyers would be a horrible way to spend the day— the aching feet, answering the same questions over and over again, and staying upbeat with one client while another client is making life miserable.

For a different person, a day spent chatting with people, getting to know what they are looking for and finding them their dream home is a ton of fun. Both of these people engage in the same activities, but they have far different responses.

To bring this into practical terms, I created this Make Money Have Fun Quadrant.

Make Money Have Fun Quadrant

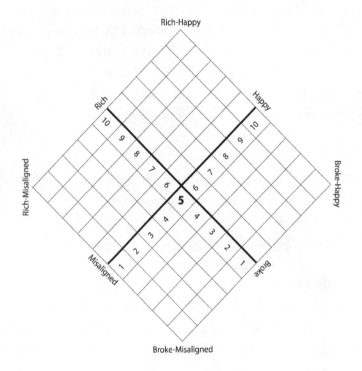

A successful entrepreneur whose business brings him joy would be in the top quadrant: Rich-Happy. Someone working at the customer service desk making $12 per hour who lives for the weekends would be in the bottom quadrant: Broke-Misaligned. Someone who makes a good living but hates his vocation would be in the left quadrant: Rich-Misaligned, and the hippie living in the woods with no job and picking berries for breakfast would be in the right quadrant: Broke-Happy.

My goal is to help you move into the top quadrant where you are Making Money and Having Fun. Here is a simple assessment to help you find which quadrant you are in today.

In the list below, circle the statement that best applies to you. Your score is the number beside that statement. When you have your number, plot it on the Make Money Have Fun Quadrant by placing a dot on the slanted line labeled Rich on top and Broke on the bottom. (See the example.)

10. Elon Musk and Jeff Bezos are your golfing buddies.

9. Your investment portfolio allows you to make generous donations to charity while continuing to grow.

8. Your investments provide enough cashflow to cover your monthly expenses.

7. You have an investment that brings you $200 in monthly cashflow.

6. You have 3 months' worth of expenses in savings.

5. Your bills are paid and you have $1000 in savings.

4. You have your own apartment but you scrape by every month, praying there are no disasters.

3. You co-lease a studio apartment with a roommate.

2. You rent a room with a shared bath.

1. You're sleeping on a friend's sofa.

In the list below, circle the statement that best applies to you. When you have your number, plot it on the slanted line labeled Happy on top and Miserable on the bottom.

10. You blast out of bed every morning eager to begin a new day—whether working or playing.
9. You enjoy your life, whether at work or having a day off.
8. You forget time, and the next thing you know, the day is over and you don't want to stop.
7. You think about your job in off hours because it challenges and excites you.
6. You feel a tingle of excitement when you begin your workday.
5. You feel bored doing your job and wish you could do something else.
4. You feel resigned to doing what you don't like because it pays the bills.
3. You feel dull and blank as you make it through your endless work day.
2. Your feet feel heavy as you head into work because it takes so much effort just to go in.
1. Your first thought of the day is, *How am I going to get through another day?*

Financial Literacy Quadrant
Make Money Have Fun Quadrant
Make Money Have Fun Quadrant Example 1
For the Example, let's say you have a score of 4 on the Rich-Broke line which begins on the bottom right, so you mark the 4. You have a score of 3 on the Happy-Misaligned line which begins on the

bottom left. After marking the 3, followed the 2 lines to where they meet. Our example ends up in the Broke-Miserable quadrant.

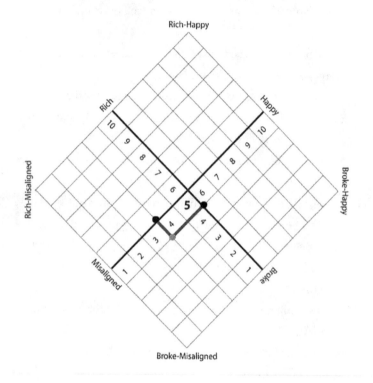

Plot both dots on the chart below to find out which Quadrant you are currently in.

Financial Literacy Quadrant

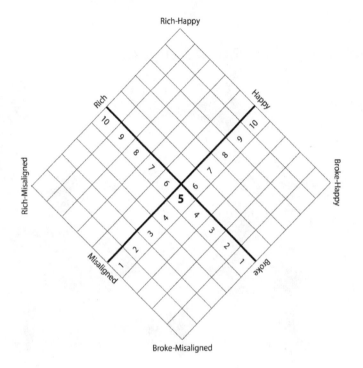

Now that you know your starting point, let's find out what makes you happy. As I'm sure you can tell by now, Make Money And Have Fun is about much more than just money. Sure, money is important as we learned in the previous chapters. Money however is probably the smallest piece. Make Money and Have Fun is about creating alignment in your life so you can be financially fulfilled. We spent time talking about the practicality of money but now we need to bring it all together in order to help you create the lifestyle you were meant to live!

SECTION 3

Have Fun

Chapter 12

IDENTIFY YOUR IDENTITY

A s you begin your journey of full alignment, you must start with your mind, the foundation. Your identity supersedes the strategy, this is a journey about who you will become first and what you will do second. Reaching the place where you are making the money you desire while having the fun you always dreamed of is created from the inside out.

Initially this might seem simple. After all, why wouldn't someone want to have fun while making money? That is a valid point but, at the same time, change isn't always pleasant while it's happening. Every choice we make creates neural pathways in our brain, the difficulty with a choice now internally becomes a matter of reconfiguring these neural pathways. You literally need to get rid of the old pathways to allow the new ones to come in, this often causes internal resistance. Externally other people might be involved, and you might encounter additional resistance from them as well as substantial repercussions. I'm bringing this up now because in this next section things start to get very personal.

To make this more actionable, I created a checklist so you can mark your progress.

❏ **Develop a high level of self-awareness and clarify your identity.**

When working with someone to discover their passions, most coaches or gurus ask, "What do you like to do?" Personally, I hate this question because it defeats the purpose. If they knew what they liked to do, they wouldn't be consulting with the coach in the first place. To me, this is the wrong question because it doesn't bring them closer to a solution. Most of us move through life unaware of our habits, and it's easy to miss important parts.

Instead, I ask, "What do you do?" and assign an exercise to generate measurable data from your life.

Here's the exercise:

Put a notepad in your pocket and track **EVERYTHING** you do every day for one week, such as…

7:30 Shower

8:00: Breakfast

8:25 Check my phone messages

Get specific. See what shows up multiple times per day and throughout the week. Circle all the habits that repeat but are non-essential (using the restroom, eating, etc. shouldn't be circled because they're essential). At the end of the week take a highlighter and highlight the top 3 repeated activities throughout that time. Finally, pick the one you'd like to do the most or combine 2 or more to begin to curate your passion.

❏ **Assess your Environment.**

Your environment is always stronger than your willpower! The first time I heard a multi-millionaire say this to me I thought "Huh?" Once he explained it my life changed from that moment forward. Like we mentioned in chapter 4, changing your environment will help you discover new opportunities, it will also help you develop new habits. Changing my environment is my number one productivity hack. Think about your habits, habits are often based on the amount of friction associated with a task, let me give an example: Imagine trying to go on a diet but your pantry is filled with cakes, cookies, marshmallows and brownies. Your fridge is stuffed with ice cream and soda, that diet is going to be near impossible right? Now, what if we changed our environment to be filled with fruits, vegetables, meat, and water, feel more doable? No matter how strong your willpower is you'll likely end up eating cakes and cookies if they're all that's in your environment. Now let's take this beyond just dieting, ask yourself: What is in your home? Do you have musical instruments? Computer parts and high-tech equipment? Sports gear? These items are all information for you to discover what your passions and habits already are. I often say to clients "show me your home and I'll show you your life." The reason is because for the most part we have already assembled our environment in direct proportion to our habits. If you want to change your habits start by changing your environment. Many millionaires I know fill their environment with what I like to call "wealth triggers" little reminders of money. I have friends who keep a stack of $100 bills on their computer desk or hang a large money canvas on the wall. Doing little things like this to reduce friction so you can be more productive as well as strategically placing reminders to keep you on track will make a world of difference in crafting your identity towards full alignment!

"Your environment is always stronger than your willpower"

❏ **Compartmentalize the tasks associated with each activity.**

When I started my Real Estate investment business, I quickly learned several steps that happened almost every time: putting out marketing, finding properties, analyzing properties, developing creative acquisition strategies, funding deals, closing deals with sellers, finding buyers, closing buyers at a profit, sharing the profits and much more. Each facet had its own set of skills.

I realized that I did not like the acquisitions part of Real Estate investing. That part seemed too time consuming—getting in your car driving to the property, talking to the owner, closing them and getting the contract signed, then showing that property to buyers and closing them. Acquisitions was not fun to me at all.

I did, however, like analyzing deals and funding them. At that moment, I was working a full time job. I had money but not much time, So, I looked at my 4 Currencies and hired someone who had time to find properties for me. I analyzed these properties and secured funding.

"I looked at my 4 Currencies and hired someone who had time."

This goes back to John Miller's QBQ technique, as you saw in Chapter 4. For example, I loved teaching martial arts, but after teaching for five years, the lifestyle of teaching four classes a day, six days a week took its toll on me. I started to feel a longing for something more.

❏ **Ask: How can I only do the parts I like from each activity?**

Like described in the previous paragraph I compartmentalized these activities and realized that the martial arts are really just a personal development program shrouded in kicks and punches. The action is fun, and kids move around and interact with others. For me the part I loved most was speaking to my classes about various aspects of personal development—motivation, inspiration, personal development and success principles.

"The martial arts are a personal development program shrouded in kicks and punches."

I asked myself another question: What if I could speak about these principles without having to run it through the medium of martial arts? So, I focused on personal development and began speaking in other places besides the karate school. Personal development led me to entrepreneurship and I fell into a community which opened a door for me to speak on a weekly basis on the same core principles I'd learned in the martial arts. Today

I speak nationally sharing the stage with people like Les Brown, Alec Stern, Dr. Greg Reid, Sir John Shin and many others.

"Personal development led me to entrepreneurship."

Going back to your assessment results and the 4 quadrants, the goal of this book is to move you into the Rich-Happy quadrant where you are Making Money and Having Fun. Let's examine next steps for the other quadrants.

If you landed in the Broke-Misaligned quadrant, the results of your tracking will give you solid information about what to focus on as you create your plan to shift your income stream to something you love. This might involve more training, networking with people who share your interests or learning more about that world and how you can make money there. Plenty of other people are already doing it, all you need to do now is find out how they are doing it.

In the Broke-Happy quadrant, most people have a mindset that money is optional and best avoided. This quadrant comes with a time limit, so it's actually an illusion. How long can living cash-free last? What happens when your health runs out, or you go through an environmental emergency?

People who have little or no money are one disaster away from a major crisis. Adjust your money mindset to see that you don't have to be 100 percent money driven, but you can use money as a platform to safeguard your future. Change the habits and ways of thinking that don't serve you. While it's true that money doesn't buy happiness, money is essential for sustaining life under most circumstances.

"People who have little or no money are
one disaster away from a major crisis."

If you're in the Rich-Misaligned quadrant, as you finish your tracking exercise, highlight those activities that are boring or distasteful to you. In the next chapter, I'll help you create a plan to Eliminate, Automate, & Delegate [EAD] the things you don't love. You'll notice a surge in energy when you can focus on things you enjoy.

Activities Checklist

❏ Develop a high level of self-awareness and clarify your identity.

❏ Assess your environment.

❏ Compartmentalize the tasks associated with each activity.

❏ Ask: How Can I only do the parts I like from each activity?

Chapter 13

ELIMINATE, AUTOMATE, & DELEGATE

E veryone has tasks they love and tasks they dread. Like I mentioned in the opening chapters, somewhere along the way, you've probably been conditioned to think that when you have tasks you don't like, the answer is to put your head down and push through them. This approach doesn't increase productivity or create growth, it only brings you closer to burnout. Imagine your life as a straight horizontal line, your "lifeline." As you move through day by day your "lifeline" will start to split. It will either split upwards towards success or downwards towards burnout. When you constantly "push" yourself to work it's only a matter of time until you burn out. On the other hand, when you're "pulled" towards your work you begin moving upward towards success. When you don't like a task, you're using a lot of extra effort with no real benefit. Like the jiu-jitsu and wrestling example from chapter 1, wrestling mentality means repeating the same move harder and harder. That's not always the best way. In jiu-jitsu, the mentality is to try different moves to see which will be successful. Wrestling has a "push" mentality whereas jiu-jitsu has a "pull" mentality. Push wears out, pull is sustainable. I think we can all agree that we've had moments in life where we dialed in and focused on a task for hours only to pick our head up and realize it's 3:22 in the morning! Conversely we've also had moments where we can't focus for longer than 3 minutes. Why is that, what makes the difference? My answer is alignment, when you dialed in you found the thing you are fully aligned with and therefore were able to give it your all. You were walking in your soul purpose and everything in your body and spirit aligned you to that purpose. The game is not to trade in the work for play, it's to choose the work you want! Full alignment doesn't mean you're working less, it's actually the exact opposite. It's about finding the work that moves you upward towards success instead of downwards towards burnout. It all comes down to your effort.

> "The game is not to trade in your work for play,
> it's to choose the work you want!"

Effort is a feeling. If you're having fun, the energy you put out seems easy, and you feel energized when you're finished. Conversely if you're working hard at something you don't enjoy, the effort seems monumental, and you feel exhausted at the end. Successful people know that the best use of their time is not plowing through drudge work. The best use of their time is to focus on the tasks that energize them and let someone or something else handle the rest. I'm often asked: "How do I know if I'm fully aligned and walking in my soul purpose?" My answer is always the same: "You feel it!" I wrote this quote in my first book "*The Revolutionary Mindset*" and it still holds true today.

> "Everyone on the face of this planet is ceaselessly searching for one thing and one thing only... a feeling!"

This means taking an honest look at what you are actually doing every day and noticing whether you enjoy that activity. Keeping a journal throughout the day can help you recognize these habits and feelings like the exercise in the last chapter. Once you have that information, you can create a plan of action for the items you do not enjoy by assigning them to one of these three categories:

1. **Eliminate:** Erasing non-essential items from your to-do list.
2. **Automate:** Using software or a system that lets you wake up in the morning to find these tasks already done.
3. **Delegate:** Handing off the tasks that don't fulfill you to someone else.

You might hire an admin to delegate, set up a Customer Relationship Management [CRM] program to automate and eliminate other activities altogether. For example, you might find that you're spending a lot of time on an aspect of marketing that has no ROI, and it's time to get rid of that dead weight while simultaneously offsetting other menial tasks to people or systems. This will increase the overall efficiency of your business and life.

"It's time to get rid of dead weight."

By automating and delegating, all the pieces still get done—faster and better than if you were doing it yourself—while your lighter load gives you the time and energy to play to the strengths that energize you, bring you joy, and potentially increased cash flow.

Judo has a philosophy of "minimum effort for maximum efficiency." In a match, this involves tripping and throws where you leverage your opponent's own momentum and save your strength. One move called *ippon* creates an instant win with a full-on throw where you launch the person with minimum effort by maximizing your efficiency. You want to adopt this same idea in your business.

"Use minimum effort for maximum efficiency."

When you understand the power of leveraging effort, you'll develop a practice of quickly shifting off those things that hold you back. Getting help these days is easy and affordable using platforms like *Fiverr.com* or *Upwork.com* and hiring virtual assistants [VAs]. Starting out with a simple plan, from there your business systems will develop as you grow.

I use *Fiverr.com* almost religiously. For quick and easy projects, you can engage a professional for anywhere between

$5-$120, depending on your budget. This is far and away the most efficient and inexpensive method I know for getting the job done. With unlimited revisions and twenty-four-hour delivery preferences, you can get your tasks done in short order and, most importantly, find a potential repeat "employee."

"Get your tasks done in short order and find a repeat 'employee.'"

One of my favorite Fiverr hacks is negotiating ongoing work. I often hand off repetitive projects to Fiverr where I can get a discount for bulk work when it comes to tasks that are repetitive and consistent.

Repetitive Vs. Consistent

Repetitive tasks need constant attention, but they appear sporadically, such as replying to emails. Consistent tasks appear at the same date and time per week or month, such as a newsletter or monthly invoicing. If you don't enjoy them, delegate or automate.

"One of my favorite Fiverr hacks is negotiating ongoing work."

As your business starts to grow, and you find yourself with a large quantity of "grunt work," I recommend upgrading from Fiverr to a personal VA. A VA is well worth the cost when you consider the ROI they can provide for your business. When it comes to hiring, I always have the same thought process: If it costs me X to make 3X, I'll repeat that process as often as I can. Putting numbers behind this: if I spend $1000 a month for a VA and I make $3000 a month because of his or her help, I would gladly bump my budget up as high as I can while maintaining the 3X return. I recommend reading *"The 4 Hour Workweek"* by Tim Ferriss to get the full run down on VA's and automated businesses.

> "I would gladly bump my budget up as high as I can while maintaining the 3X return."

A colleague told me a story recently about how she was on a campaign to grow her business by attending both local networking meetings and conferences across the country. She collected business cards from dozens of people. She made notes on those cards and placed them into labeled plastic bags for follow up.

However, once she got back to the office, her workload kept her from following up. Those plastic bags started filling up one corner of her desk. She kept adding to the pile but not following up.

One day, she realized that she was, literally, leaving a lot of money on the table. She wrote up a couple of email templates and hired a Virtual Assistant for $12/hour to follow up for her. The VA had one task: contact every email address on those business cards and schedule phone appointments with the business owner.

In one month, that small business increased by 5X. She paid the VA $360 that first month and increased her income by $4000. That's the power of leveraging someone else's time to increase your ROI. Through delegation, automation and leveraging you can maximize your efficiency by bringing on other people and systems to work for you.

Let's put this into practice.

Exercise:

Taking the activities list from your tracking exercise in the last chapter, here are your next steps:

Make Money & Have Fun Checklist

❏ Develop a high level of self-awareness and clarify your identity.

❏ Assess your environment.

❏ Compartmentalize the tasks associated with each activity.

❏ Next to each task place a Dollar Sign [$] or a Zero [0] to indicate whether that activity is making money or not.

❏ Go through the list again and add a happy face ☺ or a sad face ☹ to indicate whether you're having fun while doing this activity or not.

❏ Now move on to the EAD Chart below.

❏ Place All tasks with a 0 and ☹ in the "Eliminate" section, if possible.

❏ Place all Tasks with a $ and ☹ in the "Delegate" or "Automate" section.

❏ Tasks with a 0 and ☺ are hobbies, not businesses. Evaluate whether to continue that activity, and if so, how much time to allocate to it.

❏ Tasks with $ and ☺ are where you can Make Money and Have Fun. These are what you should personally focus on in your business.

Make Money & Have Fun Task List

_____   _____

_____   _____

_____   _____

_____   _____

_____   _____

_____   _____

_____   _____

_____   _____

_____   _____

_____   _____

_____   _____

_____   _____

_____   _____

_____   _____

_____   _____

_____   _____

Divide and Conquer Worksheet

Taking the results of your Make Money & Have Fun Task List on the previous page, divide all Sad Face ☹ items into the below sections:

Automate $ + ☹   Delegate $ + ☹

Eliminate 0 + ☹

Head over to: makemoneyandhavefun.com/blueprint to get a digital copy of this filter along with the other exercises in this section.

Chapter 14

THE NUMBER 1 KEY
TO ALL SUCCESS

After reading the last chapter you might say to yourself, "Okay, I've got this. All I have to do is compartmentalize my tasks and put them through the EAD filter." Well, it's not quite that simple.

When I began my reading escapade with the book "The Total Money Makeover" Dave Ramsey laid out a path that taught average people how to be millionaires in their late 60's and 70's. It's not a wrong message but I never wanted to be average. I wanted to know how I could achieve the same results in a fraction of the time.

We constantly hear stories of relatively young people with extraordinary results and I became obsessed with finding the answer to this question: "How can I shorten the learning curve and achieve massive results in a relatively short period of time?"

This question permeated my thoughts and I searched relentlessly for the answer until one day I found it!

Once I discovered this "secret to success" I created a 45 minute keynote with the same title as this chapter. It quickly became my most popular keynote. How did I discover this secret? Well like most profound findings this one came in the most unlikely of places.

During my reading marathon I stumbled upon a book called *The Game*. For anyone familiar with this book you likely just judged me harshly. For those uninitiated this book perhaps the most popular book on the pickup arts and how to pick up girls. At the time I'd read it to learn about social interaction and human dynamics (although the rest of it was a nice bonus). Reading through those 500-plus pages, I found a lesson that I never saw coming.

Sure the lessons and teachings about pickup arts and social dynamics were interesting but there was something else I found even more fascinating. See "*The Game*" is really an autobiography of the author, Neil Strauss, who documents his journey through the society of pick-up arts. As a writer for the *New York Times*, Strauss received an assignment to write a piece on the topic, so he began his research and went further down the rabbit hole than, perhaps, even he expected.

He started with a seminar which led to more seminars, to books, to courses, to coaches, to mentors, to live experiences and ultimately to becoming a highly sought-after coach, mentor and teacher himself. He ended up traveling the world making top dollar to teach this stuff. Here's the fascinating part: Strauss went from an unskilled, naive student to a well-paid, influential guru in only 2 years… 2 YEARS!

When I first read this, I couldn't believe it. How can someone go from zero skills and knowledge to a paid professional in only 2 years? Curiosity burned inside me, so I studied Strauss to discover his secret. What did he do differently from most other people? Let me answer that question with a story:

Let's imagine for a minute your burning desire and number one goal in life is to become an Olympic Swimmer. You wake up in the morning and immediately hop in your car and drive to the nearest community pool. You get out of your car carrying a bag filled with thermometers, glass tubes and pH testers. You spend three hours analyzing the water walking around the perimeter and occasionally sticking your toe in.

Afterwards, you drive to every sporting goods store in the area and research the best bathing suit to buy. Ten hours later, you go to bed and do more of the same the next day. Let me ask you a question before I continue. "If this is how you train to be an Olympian, what are your chances of making it to the Olympics?" Exactly... NONE! Let me say this as clearly as I can. If you want to be successful you have to get wet!

"If you want to be successful you have to get wet!"

The water in this story, if you can't tell, is a metaphor. Forget being an Olympic Swimmer for a minute, if you want to achieve success in anything you have to get wet! I define the number one key to all success as "Purposeful Immersion." These two words were chosen very carefully. The first word "purposeful" means intentional, deliberate, and definitive. It's why I waited until now to write this chapter instead of putting it in the beginning of the book. You need to find your purpose first before you can purposefully immerse yourself in anything. Which brings us to the second word "immersion" notice I didn't say touch, contact, or scrape. Immersion is full on, it's deep and engulfing. There's no mistaking immersion because it's complete and all in. Like that moment you jump in the air over the pool, when you land you will have no choice but to get wet. Again the water is a metaphor, this same mentality must be taken with any goal. I like to ask myself the question: "Am I standing in 12 feet of water right now?" I know it's impossible to stand in 12 feet of water and not get wet. Look at your own goal and determine what would be the "immersion equivalent" how can you stand in 12 feet of water with your goal?

Whatever your vision, the thing that lights you up and gets you going in the morning, don't waste another second. Jump in! Stop distracting yourself with the petty details because you want to avoid the hard work. And, by the way, if you are avoiding the hard work, maybe you need to take another look at the last chapter and find something else that truly lights you up. If you love something, you'll have no problem diving in.

> "Those who are interested will do what's convenient,
> but those who are committed will do whatever it takes."

Someone who is interested in becoming an Olympic swimmer might walk around the pool, looking at the water and imagining what it would be like to get wet. Someone who is committed will jump right in and get to work.

We do this so often. I've even done it myself where we set our mind on a vision and then dabble in it. Dabbling will never get you to your goal. You will come up short every time.

As I said before, one of the biggest myths I've seen is the catch phrase: "Do what you love and you'll never work a day in your life." Frankly, that's just not true. I would rephrase it to: "Do what you love and you'll work every single day of your life, but it will no longer feel like work."

> "Do what you love, and you'll work every single day of your life, but it will no longer feel like work."

Show up for class every day, not just some days. Arrive early and stay late. Network with people who are already where you want to go. Ask them for advice, suggestions and strategies. Purchase additional books on the topic. Become the person you want to be like Neil Strauss did. He didn't just stop after one course, book or coach, he went deep and fully immersed himself creating extraordinary results in rapid time. I found that the members in my mastermind who go above and beyond and perform this same way are the ones with the greatest results.

Become so fully immersed in your purpose that it's impossible for you to do anything but succeed. When I first started out as a Real Estate investor, I went above and beyond with my training. I read books, researched topics and hobnobbed with Real Estate millionaires. When people asked me what I did, I'd say, "I'm a Real Estate investor," even when I didn't yet purchase a house. I became who I wanted to be by immersing myself in my purpose. Everything that we want must first become real in our head before it can manifest itself in our life!

> "Get so fully immersed in your purpose
> that it's impossible for you to do anything but succeed."

Neil Strauss didn't hit Google and copy down some quick facts. He invested his time, his money and did whatever it took to reach his goal.

When you have this level of commitment, you will embrace a lifelong journey of personal development with the courage to go wherever that takes you. Your comfort zone will change. You will form new habits and stop old ones. You will break up old thought patterns. You will see yourself and every aspect of your life in new ways.

> "You will see yourself and every aspect of your life in new ways."

You might make new friends and watch old friends drift away. You might have to deal with some setbacks while you strap on your jetpack, but it will all be part of your path to Making Money and Having Fun!

Chapter 15

ATTAIN MASTERY

N ow that you've got your mindset work done, you've narrowed down your topic and you're full-on, 100 percent committed to your purpose. Now, let's take some time to maximize your progress toward your goals.

By this point I think you understand that in order to become more valuable you need to continually learn and grow. However, I want to go a little deeper here.

Learning means adding more knowledge to what you already have in various areas in your life, such as money, business, skills, investing, and on and on. Those of us on the path of personal development are continuously adding information in many areas.

Any discussion on learning begins with what you already know. I want to share with you a concept that revolutionized my way of thinking about knowledge and mastery. Take a look at this info-graphic:

All Knowledge

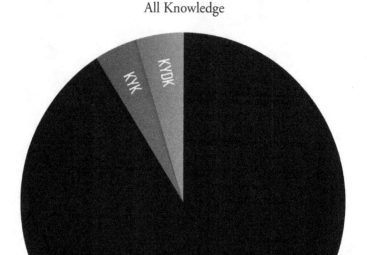

This circle represents all available knowledge in the universe. The 2 small slivers represent two different areas of you:

1. the things you know
2. the things you don't know.

Subsequently this means the remaining space in the circle represents all the things that you don't know you don't know, or what could be referred to as "your blind spot."

1. **KYK: You know you know.**

   This is the smallest slice of the pie. It contains the segment of knowledge where you feel confident. You know you can speak English or drive a car. You know you can teach your child to tie their shoes.

2. **KYDK: You know you don't know.**

   This slice contains the body of knowledge that you know you don't know. You know you don't know how to fly a plane or speak Hindi. You know you can't play the piano or build a house with your own hands.

3. **DKYDK: You don't know you don't know.**

   Everyone has a massive blind spot. Those who realize the blind spot exists are much further along than those who think they know it all and continue to stumble around on the edge of their sliver of knowledge. Simply by realizing that enormous unknowns are out there, you've experienced huge growth toward mastery. This might not feel comfortable, but it is a giant step forward. This is why billionaires always have a team of advisors who help them make decisions.

> "This is why billionaires always have a team of advisors to help them make decisions."

The key to attaining mastery is to continually expand your KYK and KYDK sliver while simultaneously making your blind spot smaller and smaller. Going through this process is the game of mastery. Anyone who joins my mastermind either has this mindset engrained in them before joining or quickly develops it just by being in proximity with others who are thinking this way. The power of proximity helps them achieve their goals even faster than they could by themselves.

Like my mastermind members, we all have a lot to learn. You can shorten your road to mastery by increasing your learning capacity while decreasing your learning curve. The infographic below will walk you through some proven tactics that will help you learn quicker with less effort.

"You can shorten your road to mastery by increasing your learning capacity while decreasing your learning curve."

The Cone of Learning

After 2 weeks, we tend to remember...

Involvement

10% of what we READ	Reading	P
20% of what we HEAR	Hearing Words	A S
30% of what we SEE	Seeing	S I
50% of what we SEE & HEAR	Watching a Movie / Looking at an Exhibit / Watching a Demonstration / Seeing It Done on Location	V E
70% of what we SAY	Participation in a Discussion / Giving a Talk	A C
90% of what we DO	Doing a Dramatic Presentation / Simulating the Real Experience / Doing the Real Thing	T I V E

During the 1960's an educator by them name of Edgar Dale began creating "The Cone of Experience" though I prefer to call it "The Cone of Learning." Studying this has helped me shorten my learning curve, my hope is it will do the same for you. As you can see by the cone, actively engaging with information is the best way to retain it. After two weeks, you will remember 90% of what you've learned if you physically work with it, if you simulate doing it or if you act it out on stage.

You can retain 70% by participating in a discussion or presenting a seminar on the topic. Think of the benefit of doing both of these—performing a demonstration followed by a group discussion about it.

Activity Stacking

One of my mastery hacks involves taking this cone one step further and stacking the top layers of learning to increase it's benefit. For example let's say you want to become a master at sales. You call another sales friend to help you out and you present sales pitches to each other in front of an audience of sales people. Afterwards, you all have a group discussion about the presentations.

You are actively engaging with the material by simulating the real experience [90% retention] and participating in a discussion about it [70% retention]. Now let's go even further and say someone in the room records the simulation for you to review [adding 50% retention for a total of 210% retention]. Stacking the activities exponentially increases the value.

"Stacking the activities exponentially increases the value."

Imagine the retention rate if you read a book in the morning, watch a movie on the same topic in the afternoon, then in the evening you give a demonstration and hold a group discussion about what happened. Video the demonstration with the discussion and watch the recorded video the next day. This is full-on Purposeful Immersion as we discussed in the last chapter with a little learning hack for an extra boost.

Now picture taking one day each week to perform at that level, with other activities on the other six days. Your mastery would skyrocket like it did for Neil Strauss.

Exercise:

1. To increase your KYK and KYDK slices of the pie, engage in something that has no connection to anything you've ever done before. Who knows it might just change your life.

2. List 3 new areas you can engage in to stretch your knowledge base:

   (Examples: cooking class, music festival, etc.)

   a. _____

   b. _____

   c. _____

3. Make a list of friends and mentors who can be on your team of advisors. (Try to pick friends and mentors who have already achieved the results you're seeking.)

   a. _____

   b. _____

   c. _____

Create a plan to make your learning quicker and easier, including as many of these as possible:

- Active engagement
- Attending a seminar
- Participating in a simulation
- Participating in a discussion
- Reading
- Listening to an audio
- Teaching someone else
- Writing about a topic
- Watching a movie

(This is a great exercise for all the tasks you listed as hobbies in the EAD Filter perviously)

Using this technique, you can branch out to acquire more and more learning in areas that intrigue you, that you might have wished you had time for but didn't see how up until now. This practice alone opens worlds and, thus, opens more opportunities.

Chapter 16

THE BIG QUESTION

When someone builds an empire, first they have to dig a really big hole and lay a foundation. That's what I've been doing up until now. I've jostled your mindsets, smashed through your comfort zone and brought giant unknowns into your field of vision. Let's take a breath and check in before going on to Section 4.

Are you still focusing on the same purpose as when we began this journey together? Have your answers changed? Have they expanded? This chapter contains activities and space for you to work, so, find a pen and spend the next few minutes going through the exercises below.

Make sure you do all the steps. Skipping ahead will short circuit your growth. We are about to launch into Section 4 where everything pulls together. You need to be clear on your objectives to get the most benefit from it.

** By the way, this chapter was the impetus for the "Make Money & Have Fun Blueprint." Go to makemoneyandhavefun. com/blueprint to get as many free copies as you need so you can always go back and do these exercises again. **

Step 1. Where are you?

Write your passion and purpose in one sentence on the lines below. If you're still unclear, return to Section 1 for some introspection and ask yourself the Big Question: "What can I fully immerse myself into without getting bored or tired?"

_____

_____

_____

_____

Does your current lifestyle allow you to fully immerse in your passion and purpose? How do the 5 Pillars of Life show up in your life right now? For example, if your passion is fitness training does the Physical Pillar currently rank high in your life? If not, this is where you begin bringing your life into alignment with what you want. We will get to that in the next step.

Below, rank each pillar on a scale from 1-10 for the weight you currently place on each area. Fill in each blank space with your number.

Here are the 5 Pillars again. How important is each one to you on a scale of 1-10, with 10 being the most important? Write that number before each pillar.

Rate each pillar below:	List pillars in order of importance:
_____ Physical	_____
_____ Mental	_____
_____ Emotional	_____
_____ Spiritual	_____
_____ Financial	_____

In column 2, rewrite the 5 pillars, ranking them from highest to lowest.

Go back to Chapter 6 to refresh your memory on how you ranked the 5 Pillars at that time and compare this to how you rank them now. Have they changed as you've gone through this discovery?

Step 2. Where do you want to go?

When you are clear on the 5 Pillars, take the Make Money and Have Fun Quadrant assessment again by circling statements in the lists below that best apply to you. This time, use two different colors to show where you are now and where you want to be. For example, use green for where you want to go and red for where you are now.

On the scale from Rich to Broke, where would you say you fall in the list below?

Rich-Broke Line

10. Elon Musk and Jeff Bezos are your golfing buddies.
9. Your investment portfolio allows you to make generous donations to charity while continuing to grow.

8. Your investments provide enough cashflow to cover your monthly expenses.

7. You have an investment that brings you $200 in monthly cashflow.

6. You have 3 months' worth of expenses in savings.

5. Your bills are paid and you have $1000 in savings.

4. You have your own apartment but you scrape by every month, praying there are no disasters.

3. You co-lease a studio apartment with a roommate.

2. You rent a room with a shared bath.

1. You're sleeping on a friend's sofa.

On the scale from Happy to Miserable where are you and where do you want to be in the list below?

Happy-Miserable Line

10. You blast out of bed every morning eager to begin a new day—whether working or playing.

9. You enjoy your life, whether at work or having a day off.

8. You forget time, and the next thing you know, the day is over and you don't want to stop.

7. You think about your job in off hours because it challenges and excites you.

6. You feel a tingle of excitement when you begin your workday.

5. You feel bored doing your job and wish you could do something else.

4. You feel resigned to doing what you don't like because it pays the bills.

3. You feel dull and blank as you make it through your endless work day.

2. Your feet feel heavy as you head into work because it takes so much effort just to go in.

1. Your first thought of the day is, *How am I going to get through another day?*

Plot both points on the X lines below. The Rich-Broke line begins on the bottom right. The Happy-Miserable line begins on the bottom left. Your colored dots show where you are now and where you want to go. See the example below.

Financial Literacy Quadrant Example 2

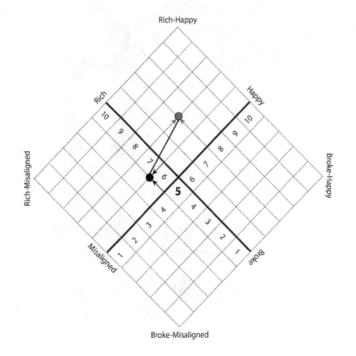

Let's say you are currently at 4,6 in the Rich-Miserable Quadrant but you want to be at 7, 7 in the Rich-Happy Quadrant. The connecting line shows your goal path.

Although this person might feel like they are far from their goal, they could be closer than they think. By improving their happiness by two points, they would be in the Rich-Happy Quadrant and could continue to make improvements from a better place.

Financial Literacy Quadrant

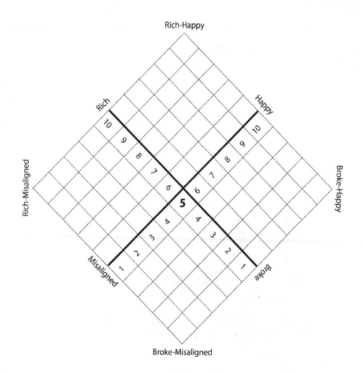

After you plot your points, draw a line joining the two dots. Notice how many points lie between your current status and the Rich-Happy Quadrant.

Next, create an action plan and with specific steps, starting with the 5 Pillars. In the blanks below, set goals for the 5 Pillars of Life that will take you closer to full immersion in your passion and purpose.

Physical (For Example, start a gym membership, healthier eating)

_____

_____

_____

_____

Mental (For Example, take a course, hire coach)

_____

_____

_____

_____

Emotional (For Example, spend more family time, volunteering)

_____

_____

_____

_____

Spiritual (For Example, spiritual practice, meditation)

_____

_____

_____

_____

Financial (For Example, update my budget, increase my credit limits)

_____

_____

_____

_____

In order to open space for your above goals, use the Make Money Have Fun Checklist to see where you can Eliminate, Automate or Delegate activities that currently weigh you down and keep you from the Rich-Happy Quadrant.

Make Money & Have Fun Checklist

❏ Develop a high level of self-awareness and clarofy your identity.

❏ Assess your Environment.

❏ Compartmentalize the Tasks associated with each activity.

❏ List individual tasks for each activity on the Make Money & Have Fun Task List below.

❏ Next to each task place a Dollar Sign [$] or a Zero [0] to indicate whether that activity is making money or not.

❏ Go through the list again and add a happy face ☺ or a sad face ☹ to indicate whether you're having fun while doing this activity or not.

❏ Now move on to the EAD Filter below.

❏ Place All tasks with a 0 and ☹ in the "Eliminate" section, if possible.

❏ Place all Tasks with a $ and ☹ in the Delegate or Automate section.

❏ Tasks with a 0 and ☺ are hobbies, not businesses. Evaluate whether to continue that activity, and if so, how much time to allocate to it.

❏ Tasks with $ and ☺ are where you can Make Money and Have Fun. These are what you should personally focus on in your business.

Make Money & Have Fun Task List

Next to each task, in the small blank place a $ or 0 and a ☺ or ☹ to indicate whether this task is Making Money and whether it is fun.

_____ _____

_____ _____

_____ _____

_____ _____

_____ _____

_____ _____

_____ _____

_____ _____

_____ _____

_____ _____

_____ _____

_____ _____

_____ _____

_____ _____

_____ _____

_____ _____

EAD FilterCompartmentalize the activities from the Task List that have sad faces.

Automate $ + ☹   Delegate $ + ☹

Eliminate 0 + ☹

Step 3. Create a detailed action plan.

With each exercise you are narrowing down your tasks and creating a plan to reach your goal of Making Money and Having Fun. Here are more useful tools to help you get clear on your next steps.

QBQ Questions

When you create action steps, ask QBQ questions that begin with *what* or *how*, then add *I* and an action. Take the QBQ process to 3 levels or more until you have defined a clear action. This is a funnel consisting of the Question, QBQ1 and QBQ2. Better questions will give you better answers

For example:

Question

How can I make more money?

QBQ1

How much more money do I need to make?

QBQ2

What do I want to make money for? (an actionable amount)

Use these lines below to create your own QBQ's:

Question

_____

_____

_____

_____

_____

_____

QBQ1

_____

_____

_____

_____

_____

_____

_____

_____

QBQ2

_____

_____

_____

_____

_____

_____

_____

_____

Now that you have more specific goals, consider how you might use the 4 Currencies (money, time, knowledge and relationships) to reach your goals. In the chart below, make a plan to maximize the 4 Currencies to gain access to what you need.

The 4 Currencies

Have _____ Money   Need _____

Who has this currency? _____

How can I connect with them? _____

Have _____ Time   Need _____

Who has this currency? _____

How can I connect with them? _____

Have_____ Knowledge Need _____

Who has this currency? _____

How can I connect with them? _____

Have_____ Relationships Need _____

Who has this currency? _____

How can I connect with them? _____

As a Reader, this is the place where most people would skim and skip to get to the end of the book without taking action. This is the point that takes me back to that moment in 2018 when my Real Estate business was collapsing in front of my eyes, and I had a choice to make:

Do I keep going or do I give up? That very second, I only said one thing in my mind: "This is the point where most people would give up, but I don't want to be most people."

"Persistence is the antidote to your worst case scenario!"

All you have left now is your choice...

SECTION 4

Bridge the Gap

Chapter 17

MONETIZE YOUR PASSION

In this final section I want to focus on taking your passion, which we crafted in the last section, and attaching it to dollars so it can go from just a fun activity to an income producing business. What I've found is that typically people fall into one of 2 categories at this point: 1.They don't know how to monetize their passion. 2. They don't think that their passion can be monetized. My hope is that this chapter debunks both of these myths for you. Let's start with number 2.

You might think your passion is too "obscure" or "uncommon" or "weird" or "whatever," fact is It doesn't matter because you absolutely can monetize it! If you have one of these "not so common" passions you would fall into the category of what I like to call "the unconventional entrepreneur." Great news, you're in luck because there are many more like you out there, let me show you.

In Gary Vaynerchuk's book, *Crush It*, he says that if your passion in life is collecting bottle caps, you can make money selling bottle caps. All you have to do is find the other five dozen people on the planet who also love bottle caps and sell to them. You can also sell documentation about bottle cap designers and designs, information about where to find bottle caps and ideas for how to display them…just for starters.

Multi-millionaire skateboarder Tony Hawk loved skateboarding. His friends and family told him he was nuts and he'd never make a living doing what he loved. At nineteen years old, Tony was making $150,000 a year! Now he's a worldwide celebrity who basically writes his own incredibly hefty paychecks.

YouTuber Casey Neistat was a filmmaker in Hollywood, but felt misaligned. He realized this wasn't his passion, so he pivoted and started making vlogs of his daily life on Youtube. Today he has over 10 million subscribers and typically receives close to 1 million views within an hour of posting a video.

Casey is not the only one, today millions of people have built successful businesses from YouTube, filming themselves doing what they love. But it doesn't stop at Youtube look at the rise of monetization around social media. Instagram influencers, Tiktok gurus, Facebook, Twitter, Clubhouse, the list goes on and guess what, it's not done yet. We live in an age where making money online is commonplace and in many cases requires low to no barriers to entry.

Full time, online entrepreneurs come in all sorts—vloggers, bloggers, artists, digital nomads, influencers, etc. What they all have in common is a passion and a vision for making money while having fun.

"What they all have in common is a passion
and a vision for making money while having fun."

You might also have a natural ability that you are still over-looking. For example, a friend of mine loves to laugh. She has an infectious laugh, and she's not afraid to use it. Someone acting in a comic play asked her to sit in the audience during rehearsals, so the cast could hear her laughing and know when they were actually funny. After that, she started getting free theater tickets because word got out that her infectious laugh loosens up an audience. They become a better crowd and the cast gives a better performance. Does she enjoy it? Sure. She loves to laugh.

I love to speak and teach; therefore I stand on stages and write books like this. The information I'm sharing with you is the same process I went through to get here. I figured out that I could impact others by writing and speaking, then I figured out how to get paid to do it, and the process works the same for anyone including you.

"You might also have a natural ability that you are still overlooking."

The Big Question: What do you love enough for full immer-sion? What could you dive into for the next ten years and never get tired or bored? Today's technology offers a smorgasbord of opportunities for ways you can make money while having fun like I mentioned earlier.

If you've achieved a level of mastery at your favored skill or activity, you can compete, hold demonstrations and teach sem-inars. You can create a course and put it up on Udemy, Skillshare or many other online platforms almost instantly. But even if you're not that great, here are some ways you can still make a living doing what you love:

- Interview successful people who do what you love and put those interviews out as videos, articles, social media posts or compile them into a book.
- Become a reporter for the latest news and events about your passion. Start a podcast. Build your following. From your platform sell ads, offer affiliate promotions and add merchandise.
- Create tutorials for beginners and place them on Skillshare or Udemy.
- Hold spoof contests in your backyard, a park or on the beach. Post the videos across social media.
- Start a man-on-the-street vlog interviewing random people on their views about your topic.
- Publish a yearly ranking of who is best in your field. Interview those people.
- Set up an ecommerce site where people can buy, sell and trade products and merchandise.

Remember, you are building a business, so stay alert for ways to monetize in all 4 Currencies. A lot of people dabble in the above steps, so they treat their passion as a hobby. They don't immerse themselves, and they fail to monetize. You want both dollar signs and smiley faces, so keep your eye on the prize.

"Stay alert for ways to monetize in all 4 Currencies."

Exercise:

Take a day to yourself—no phone calls or work. Go to the train station, the coffee shop or your own basement and think about how many ways you can turn your passion into a business where you can make money while having a lot of fun.

Chapter 18

PULL THE TRIGGER

After all the introspection, all the clarity and all the preparation, one step still remains: pulling the trigger. It's easy to be an armchair expert. Getting started is where so many people put off taking action, and they use logic to back them up.

Pulling the trigger means making that phone call, launching that podcast, starting your YouTube channel, applying for your dream job, etc. It means taking real steps to make your dream happen.

If you are procrastinating, it's time to take a closer look at your internal dialog and check in on your mindset. Here are some frequently used excuses for failure to launch:

This will never work for me.

You might have a thousand reasons why you can't make money while having fun, ranging from:

"I'm not good with people."

"I'm too much of a pushover to make good deals."

"I can't _____ (write, do social media, sell anything, and on and on)."

"I'm too ___ (old, young, shy, tongue-tied, etc., etc., etc.)"

One answer covers all of the above. This is about focusing on your strengths and leveraging your weaknesses. If you hate sales, then partner with someone who loves sales. If you are a soft negotiator, let someone else handle the tough conversations while you stick with things you love to do. You always have the EAD filter in your back pocket. Don't forget you can Eliminate, Automate or Delegate whatever you don't like or you're not good at. Here's the link again to the blueprint if you want to download it for yourself: makemoneyandhavefun.com/blueprint

> "Don't forget you can Eliminate, Automate & Delegate whatever you don't like or you're not good at."

One caveat: Don't sell yourself before you're sold. If you've never had training on something and assume you won't like it, this is a mindset problem. If you've never tried, take some training and give yourself a chance. You might find out you're a natural, and you love it.

A friend of mine said for years that she didn't like sales, and she was bad at it. Then she took a job where a part of her responsibilities was sales. She had to attend a week of live training. She found out that she loved sales and made top in her region in nine months. This could be true for you, too.

> "Don't sell yourself before you're sold."

I always get off track. I'm afraid I'll get off track with this, too.

Your biggest challenge won't be creating a Make Money and Have Fun lifestyle, but staying there. Everyone gets off track. Studies show that airline pilots spend more than 90% of their time course correcting, yet they reach their goal on time. Like them, you'll spend 90% of your efforts course correcting. However, that's not a flaw, it's the way life is. When you reach your destination, you'll realize it was all worth it!

> "Your biggest challenge won't be entering the Make Money and Have Fun lifestyle, but staying there."

People love routines and comfort zones. That's why it's so easy to end up with your calendar overloaded and your passion drifting into the background. Imagine that your life has two speedometers, and you need to continuously check both of them; this is similar to if you were flying a plane or driving a car.

Imagine that one speedometer measures fun, and the other measures income. Whatever your venture, if both gauges come off of 10, your car will veer off the road, and you'll end up in the ditch. You might make money but have no fun, or you might have fun but make no money.

If you start dreading some activities, your fulfillment gauge is going toward E. If you're not making money, your income gauge will land in the red.

Your income equals your sustainability. When you keep them both at 10, you are in full alignment. You'll wake up with a surge of energy and an eagerness for your day. You can also sustain yourself indefinitely. Make a regular habit of checking your gauges. When you spot yourself drifting, you can quickly pull things back in line.

I know I'll screw up.

Tony Robbins tells a story about playing golf. He hired a professional trainer and went to the green for months, finally he thought he was getting the hang of it when he had a terrible day on the green. We've all had days like this but Tony was totally frustrated he felt like his ball consistently landed closer to the pro-shop than the hole. His coach was silent for a while until he saw Tony's frustration getting to him and he finally spoke up. "You're only a couple of millimeters off" he said. "Could have fooled me!" an infuriated Tony retorted back. His coach knew it was time for the lesson "When you struck that last ball" he said "if you had just adjusted your club by 1-2 millimeters when you made contact you would have had a hole in one." At that moment Tony realized that 1 millimeter put the ball off on a wide trajectory, so by the time it reached the hole it was way off. The same is true with everything in life, like I wrote in my first book: "One Millimeter of change can create a mile of difference!"

There is hope: Just make a 1 mil change, and you'll see a mile of difference in your life.

"1 millimeter of change can make a mile of difference in your life!"

When I was training in jiu-jitsu, my instructor shared the four stages of competency with me:

Unconsciously incompetent—I have no idea what I'm doing.

Consciously incompetent—I'm really bad at this.

Consciously competent—I have to concentrate to do this.

Unconsciously competent—I do this automatically, no thought required.

My jiu-jitsu instructor told me that a new student coming in basically gets beat up for a while. Every time they come in for training, they get destroyed. They are Unconsciously Incompetent and have no idea what they are doing.

This happens week after week. Eventually, the student will go to the instructor and say, "I've been here a long time. Why am I still getting destroyed?"

When that happens, the instructor can see that this student is now Consciously Incompetent, they are realizing how bad they are. The instructor says, "I'm so happy to see you're growing so much!"

The student says, "Huh? I'm not growing. I'm getting destroyed."

The teacher replies, "The fact that you brought it up shows that you recognize your incompetency. Now you can really begin to learn."

This same progression happens in the Make Money and Have Fun lifestyle. Once you begin to realize how much you need to change, you can begin taking steps to get better. While it isn't always comfortable, it is a step forward.

How can I start something while I still work a fulltime job?

If you truly love what you're doing, spending nights and weekends doing that won't be as hard as you think. You'll feel a rush of excitement when you have a chance to do what you love. If you don't feel that rush, that organic motivation, maybe you should take another look at what you're doing. Maybe it's not your true passion.

Another possibility is to look at which tasks you dread. If you love creating crafts and selling them on Etsy but you dread the packing and shipping, maybe you should find someone else to pack and ship for you.

> *"Those who are committed will do whatever it takes.*
> *Those who are interested will do what's convenient."*
> ~John Assaraf

I went through this myself in Real Estate investing. One of the career paths in Real Estate investing is called wholesaling. Wholesalers put a property under contract, then they sell that contract to an end buyer for a fee. At closing, three people are typically at the table--the seller, the wholesaler and the end buyer.

Real Estate wholesalers hustle every day. They are constantly negotiating with sellers and buyers, always looking for the next deal. For me, I find wholesaling tedious, stressful and anxiety-ridden. The thought of being a wholesaler puts a knot in my stomach.

Here's what's interesting. As a professional speaker, my tasks are virtually the same as a wholesaler. We both travel a lot, spend time on the phone negotiating deals, even the fees are in the same range. Yet, I feel exhilaration from public speaking whereas wholesaling I feel drudgery.

The feeling makes the difference. Audit your feelings and find the thing that exhilarates you. When that's the case, you won't have to push yourself out of bed on Saturday morning. You'll be up and ready to go with a spring in your step, looking forward to the day. I said it before and I'll say it again: Do what you love, and you'll work every day of your life, but it will no longer feel like work.

> "Do what you love, and you'll work every day of your life, but it will no longer feel like work."

I'm not passionate enough about anything to make money at it.

Lani Lazzari developed eczema at the age of 11. She couldn't find anything in the skincare aisles that worked for her, so she started making moisturizing sugar scrubs for sensitive skin. Friends and family with sensitive skin wanted her products. At age 17, she started Simple Sugars and ended up with a Shark-Tank deal at age 18.

Lani turned her problem into a business. If you feel you're not passionate about anything, you might be overlooking something that's become such a part of your life that you're missing a golden opportunity right in front of you.

> "You could be missing a golden opportunity right in front of you."

Combine your passions.

Sometimes combining two different areas of interest can create a new spin on a familiar topic, such as a craftsman who loves to barbeque. He starts out working with metal and ends up at barbeque competitions, selling his hand-forged knives.

Combining passions provides an unlimited number of options. For example, Mary is a special-education teacher who loves to garden. Combining her two passions, she created a program to teach beginners with no previous exposure to gardening. Not only does she spend her days doing what she loves, but she used this combination to serve a specific niche, giving her a marketing advantage.

"Combining passions can give you an advantage."

Look at specific tasks within bigger activities.

This is what I did when I was a karate instructor. After teaching karate for several years, I realized that the task I really loved was teaching personal development. I like to think of this as the second circle out on the target. Karate was the second circle. For me, the bull's eye was personal development.

Go one level deeper in your area, the thing you love doing. It's almost like creating a QBQ for your passion. What thing inside that thing do you like best?

"What thing inside that thing do you like best?"

Pull back a level and see if you'd rather get more general.

The opposite of the previous suggestion, if you have a passion that doesn't seem big enough, you could possibly get more general. In this case, what you are looking at is the bull's eye when you want to be one ring out.

For example, maybe you are involved in a direct sales company selling household products via home parties. Maybe you find home parties to be tedious. You don't like hauling product into people's homes, and you don't like late nights. If you pull back one level, maybe you'll find you enjoy training other people how to do home parties instead. When you look broader, you might find your sweet spot.

"When you look broader, you might find your sweet spot."

Play more and try new things.

If you still aren't sure what your passion is, give yourself a chance to discover something inside you that you haven't experienced yet. Take some classes, go to new places and try new things. If you watch someone else and think, "I wish I could do that," take note and give it a try.

"Give yourself a chance to discover something inside you that you haven't experienced yet."

List some thoughts of where you could go with your passion and how to take it to the next level if you haven't yet dialed in.

_____

_____

_____

_____

_____

_____

_____

Chapter 14

ACTION HACKS

As you establish new routines, new habits and new ways of engaging with the world, remember that your environment is always stronger than your willpower like we discussed in chapter 12. Most of the time, people who struggle with change are in an environment that creates obstacles for them. Prepare your home, your car and your office to streamline your success and increase your productivity. Create an environment that sets you up for success.

> "Create an environment that sets you up for success."

This means subtracting things that hold you back and adding things that support success

Motivation Precedes Action

Why was I able to sit down and read sixteen books that first year when I had never read a book before? I wanted to learn. I was motivated. The same is true for making any big changes in your life to reach your dream.

When you are walking in your soul purpose and having fun, motivation happens organically. Still, even then, sometimes you might get stuck. The thought of tackling your chaotic office and bringing it into some sort of order, the idea of meeting new people at a seminar or in a mastermind, or maybe the prospect of becoming an entrepreneur might feel like a wall you have to break down.

Because you have stepped outside your comfort zone, coming face to face with that wall is inevitable. Don't worry. You can get through it.

> "Because you have stepped outside your comfort zone,
> coming face to face with that wall is inevitable."

For example, let's say your dream of creating a career out of collecting bottle caps is waiting for you on the other side of that imaginary wall. On your side of the wall, you will stay in a job you dread. To help you break through the wall, here are some Action Hacks. Follow them, and you'll soon bust through the plaster, take out the studs and step through the wall to embrace your fully aligned life.

Minimize Friction

Podcaster and YouTuber, Thomas J. Frank puts out a lot of material on productivity. He talks about minimizing friction by removing any unnecessary steps between you and what you want to accomplish. For example, let's say you want to add half an hour at the gym to your morning routine. If you wake up and realize that your gym bag is at the back of a shelf filled with Christmas ornaments outside in the freezing cold garage, you have a lot of steps between you and success. With all those steps, how likely is it that you will roll over and catch another forty winks instead of reaching for your goal?

Minimizing friction means your gym bag is already in the car and ready to go when your alarm goes off. Your clothes wait nearby along with your keys.

If you want to create YouTube videos, set up a recording location where you can sit down, flip a switch and start filming. If you record on-the-go video, have your equipment ready to grab whenever you walk out the door. Minimizing friction is an important step toward full immersion, and full immersion is key to your success.

"Minimizing friction is an important step toward full immersion."

Set up wealth triggers.

I mentioned these before but it's worth mentioning again. Millionaire Mentor, Dan Lok gives a YouTube tour of his home where he highlights what he calls "wealth triggers." An expensive statue on his desk has a specific purpose: to keep his wealth vibration high.

Behind his desk where he can see them, he has placed items that inspire him—signed photos of his role models, inspirational icons, as well as memorabilia and family photos. He has a full room dedicated to his book library and a quiet place for his morning meditation equipped with a zero-gravity massage chair to help him get into the zone.

Dan knows that his environment is stronger than willpower, so he set up his home and office to pull himself toward the wealth he also mentors others to find.

> "Dan set up his home and office to pull himself toward the wealth he also mentors others to find."

Tony Robbins also had to create his environment before he could engage in his high-energy morning routine where he wakes up at 4:30 a.m. to drink an adrenal-support cocktail, go through his priming meditation, and workout involving a number of movements including jumping on a trampoline and a polar plunge. He sets himself up to be a global leader who inspires millions by keeping himself in top condition in all 5 Pillars of Life. Tony Robbins knows that his environment is stronger than willpower.

What about you? How can you adapt your environment to shape it for your own success?

Exercise:

List the activities that are essential to your success, not only *doing* what you need to do but also *being* who you need to be. For Tony Robbins, being who he needs to be starts with a polar plunge in the morning. For Dan Lok, being who he needs to be means starting the day with meditation and quiet. What would your best day look like?

In the first column below, list the activities throughout the entire day that are success triggers for you. In the second column, list steps to adapt your environment along with actions that will minimize friction.

_____   _____

_____   _____

_____   _____

_____   _____

_____   _____

_____   _____

_____   _____

_____   _____

_____   _____

_____   _____

_____   _____

_____   _____

_____   _____

_____   _____

_____   _____

_____   _____

_____   _____

Chapter 20
YOU'RE NOT READY

t the end of a webinar, people often come up to me and say, "I don't feel like I'm ready to do this myself. Can you do it for me?"

That's a valid question, and if you're feeling that way, too, my response is in two parts:

1. **There's no such thing as ready.**

If you're feeling like the timeline is off and you're not ready, remember, there's no such thing as ready. There's only the best you are at the current time. I see this so often with people who want to take one more class or go to one more event or read one more book.

It sounds logical to sharpen your ax before you start chopping logs, right? Actually, this is a sneaky delay tactic. Instead, take your current best and head toward the goal, picking up resources as you go. Make big moves before you're ready.

What are you not ready for? How can you get ready? If you need more information, more time, more money or more relationships, refer back to the 4 Currencies chart and think about who might have those things and how you might trade for them. You don't have to wait until you can produce them yourself.

Ready-set-go works for track-and-field races, but successful people know that *ready* is an illusion, an excuse for not pulling the trigger. The real reason is hiding below the surface.

This is another reason why I started The Make Money And Have fun Mastermind, it's designed for anybody who feels they aren't yet ready or has questions about how to grow and scale. The beauty is it's not just me who will help you on your path it's everyone in the room. If you're interested in learning more about how you can get involved head over to: makemoneyandhavefun. com/mastermind for more information.

"Successful people know that *ready* is an illusion."

You have the passion. You can get the tools you still need. The only thing holding you back at this point is your own thinking.

2. **If I did the work for you, the results would be mine, not yours.**

One of the biggest myths in our culture is that success leaves clues. However, simply following the steps of someone successful is not a surefire path to Making Money and Having Fun. What an expert did to achieve success might be something that you aren't comfortable with. They might be a Round Peg while you are a Square Peg. You can often achieve the desired result while using different methods. It's more important to focus on the result than the method.

For example: I'm not a big fan of smiling and dialing (making a ton of calls). I love sales conversations, but if you give me a sheet of phone numbers and tell me to call them, I will avoid that list as long as I possibly can. Am I a bad sales person because I can't stand calling? Not at all. It just means I'm a Square Peg, and I don't resonate with that Round Peg method.

Sometimes mentees get stars in their eyes and blindly follow their mentor. They don't resonate with the method, but they believe they have to push through the pain to get the same results. In the first place, remember push vs. pull, pushing through pain will most likely not get you those results because you have a resistance to what you're doing. In the second place, if you're pushing through, you have stepped off the Make Money and Have Fun path.

> "If you're pushing through, you have stepped off
> the Make Money and Have Fun path."

If you ask me to make a cake for you, I'll do it my way and end up with a chocolate cake when your vision was a vanilla cake. You have to live your life your own way. If not, you will end up where you don't want to be. You might be making money, but you are back to having no fun. Right back where you started.

> "You might be making money, but you are back to having no fun.
> Right back where you started."

During my 5 years as an instructor, I realized my beginning jiu-jitsu students experienced more frustration than students in any other martial art I taught. I started to look for a way to help those students, and I came up with what I call "The Puzzle Box Analogy."

It goes like this:

On your first day of class, along with your uniform and your belt imagine that you received an empty puzzle box as well. Every time you attend class you receive puzzle pieces for your puzzle box. This puzzle has no border, and no picture on the box to let you know how you're doing.

As you go through the classes, you collect the pieces and put them into your box. When you move from a white belt to a blue belt, you'll look down and realize that some pieces go together. You fit them into small clusters.

You continue receiving puzzle pieces every day. When you get to purple belt, you realize that your small clusters can now make bigger clusters.

Over the years, you still receive pieces every day. When you receive your Brown belt, you bring some clusters together and build more of your puzzle. The more mastery you achieve, the more puzzle pieces you have. Eventually, you realize that your puzzle will never be completely finished. Every day, you will continue to receive more pieces, so the puzzle will always continue to grow even through Black Belt.

This same principle applies to any area of expertise. Whenever you enter a new field of mastery, you will tend to feel frustrated at first. You want to jump in to finish the puzzle. However, that is not your job as a new student. Your job is simply to continue showing up and collecting puzzle pieces.

Although you might feel an inner drive to rush and get the puzzle done, be patient. Keep collecting puzzle pieces and putting together clusters. Eventually, you will be able to create bigger clusters and bigger sections. The goal is not to finish the puzzle, but to enjoy collecting the pieces. Recognize your constant progress.

Like jiu-jitsu, learning is a lifelong process, not simply a quick trip to a destination.

"Learning is a lifelong process, not simply a quick trip to a destination."

What could be better than living your life in flow where you're so captivated that you lose track of time?

What could be better than loving your life while enjoying the financial rewards of your work?

What could be better than days filled with fun and fulfillment where you take vacations because you want to enjoy experiences with your family, not because you're feeling burnt out?

What could be better than living life on your own terms with flexibility and the finances to enjoy whatever your heart desires?

What could be better? So, what are you waiting for?

Now it's your turn to go Make Money and Have Fun!

—Fred Posimo

A Note From the Author

This training manual might be complete, but the work is just getting started. Here are more ways to help you along your journey.

1. Text the word **blueprint** to my direct line: 215-596-1515 and I'll send you "The Make Money & Have Fun Blueprint" to help keep you on track to Making Money & Having Fun!

2. Visit my website: MakeMoneyandHaveFun.com to access even more free resources!

3. Subscribe to my YouTube channel (Fred Posimo) and check out my syndicated web show, podcast, and TV Show (The Make Money & Have Fun Show) where I interview experts every week!

4. Connect with me on Facebook, Instagram and YouTube.

5. Still have questions? Email me at fredposimo@gmail.com and I'll get back to you soon.

ABOUT THE AUTHOR

S peaker, coach, and author, Fred Posimo is a Certified Mastermind Facilitator, personally mentored by Les Brown. He is a national speaker who has shared the stage with the likes of Greg Reid, Les Brown, Tony Robbins and many more business icons.

On his syndicated podcast and TV Show "The Make Money & Have Fun Show," Fred interviews millionaire and billionaire entrepreneurs including Alec Stern, Les Brown, Sir John Shin, Dr. Greg Reid, as well as many others.

In 2017, Fred started his Real Estate investment company at age 23 and now has holdings valued at nearly half a million dollars and growing. His first two books, *The {R}Evolutionary Mindset* and *The Thought Bible* are available on Amazon.com.

He received his second-degree black belt in Kenpo karate and has taught multiple martial arts styles including but not limited to Boxing, Kickboxing, Tae-Kwon Do, Judo, Jiu-Jitsu, Muay Thai and even Wrestling to students ranging from 3½ years old to adults for over half a decade.

Fred lives in the Philadelphia area where he does two things on a daily basis: Make Money & Have Fun! Today he focuses on helping others do the same.

To book Fred for a speaking engagement, call or text 215-596-1515 or email fredposimo@gmail.com. Visit his web site at fredposimo.com to learn more.

Additional Resources

12 Rules for Life by Jordan Peterson
Crush It by Gary Vaynerchuk
Drive by Woody Woodward
QBQ! The Question Behind the Question by John Miller
Rich Dad Poor Dad by Robert Kiyosaki
The Game by Neil Strauss
The [R]evolutionary Mindset by Fred Posimo
The Total Money Makeover by Dave Ramsey

A free ebook edition is available with the purchase of this book.

To claim your free ebook edition:

1. Visit MorganJamesBOGO.com
2. Sign your name CLEARLY in the space
3. Complete the form and submit a photo of the entire copyright page
4. You or your friend can download the ebook to your preferred device

Print & Digital Together Forever.

Snap a photo   Free ebook   Read anywhere